Also available at all good book stores

9781801500630

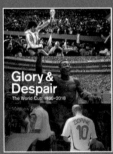
9781801501248

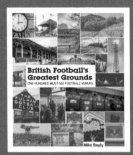
9781785316470

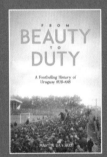
9781801501491

9781801501552

9781801503709

9781801503723

9781801501682

9781801501668

ERIC &
DAVE

ERIC & DAVE

A Lifetime of Football and Friendship

SPENCER VIGNES

First published by Pitch Publishing, 2022

Pitch Publishing
9 Donnington Park,
85 Birdham Road,
Chichester,
West Sussex,
PO20 7AJ
www.pitchpublishing.co.uk
info@pitchpublishing.co.uk

ISBN 978 1 80150 198 9

Typesetting and origination by Pitch Publishing
Printed and bound in India by Replika Press Pvt. Ltd.

CONTENTS

Also by Spencer Vignes

The Server

*A Few Good Men: The Brighton & Hove
Albion Dream Team*

The Wimbledon Miscellany

*Lost in France: The Remarkable Life and Death of Leigh
Roose, Football's First Superstar*

*The Train Kept A-Rollin': How the Train Song Changed the
Face of Popular Music*

*Bloody Southerners: Clough and Taylor's
Brighton & Hove Odyssey*

For those who play, for
those who watch, and for
those we've lost

'When you are a goalkeeper, there's no halfway.
You can be a half good player out on the
field somewhere, but you can't be a half good
goalkeeper. They, they can make mistakes all
day long. Score one goal and they're a hero.
The goalie, he – or she – can play a great game
all day. But, make one slip, and they'll say you
are hopeless. That's the way it has always been.
And that's the way it will always be.'

Eric Gill

'You don't make many friends in football. At least not close ones. But I've come to realise over the years that Eric and I are different. We've been through so much, both together and as individuals. And we're still here. After all this time, getting on for 70 years from when we first met, we're still here.'

Dave Hollins

INTRODUCTION

THIS IS a story that came dangerously close to never being told.

In May 2020, in my capacity as a freelance writer of umpteen years' standing, I interviewed a man called Eric Gill – over the phone rather than face to face, what with Covid-19 having paralysed society. Way back when, Eric had been one of the finest goalkeepers in Britain, a Londoner who made headlines around the world by appearing in 247 consecutive matches for Brighton & Hove Albion between February 1953 and February 1958, equalling a Football League record for goalies in the process (the curious among you will notice use of the word 'equalling' there – that, my friends, is a story in itself).

Given football's intensely physical nature in those days, that achievement took some doing. Besides keeping the ball out of the net, goalkeepers also had to make do with being, to all intents and purposes, beaten black and blue every week by opposing centre-forwards, along with anyone else on the field of play who fancied having a go. Look up 'brutal' in the *Oxford English Dictionary* and it will say 'the art of goalkeeping circa 1875 to 1960'. Or at least it should.

I'd never spoken to Eric before, but I knew of him. Growing up in Sussex during the 1970s into the 1980s and supporting Brighton & Hove Albion, I heard talk among older fans stood around me at home matches of the goalkeeper to beat all other goalkeepers, the one who'd played year upon year without missing so much as a single match. Being a young keeper myself, albeit of limited potential, I couldn't help but be impressed. Here was a bona fide sepia superhero straight out of Pathé News – and he'd played in my position for my favourite club.

However, it wasn't only Eric's story that interested me. Behind every first-choice goalkeeper, there's an understudy, the poor sod who has to wait their turn until the main man or woman falls from grace, or breaks their fingers, or gets spirited away by another club. Eric's unbroken run had lasted five years. People do less for murder, yet someone with the patience of a saint must have waited for his chance.

… and waited.

… and waited.

In time, I learned the identity of that saint – Dave Hollins. Signed as a teenager in 1955 to replace a couple of other goalkeepers who'd grown tired of watching the paint dry, Dave got his hands dirty in Brighton's reserve team for three years until, out of the blue, the seemingly immovable Eric developed flu. Into the breach Dave stepped for three matches, doing well but nevertheless making way once Eric was fit again.

Six months later came another opportunity. Alas, this time things didn't work out quite so hunky-dory. As I write, Middlesbrough 9 Brighton & Hove Albion 0 remains Middlesbrough's record league win and Brighton's heaviest-ever defeat. And Brian Clough – yes, that Brian Clough – scored five of them.

At this stage you could easily have forgiven Dave had he traded goalkeeping for, in the words of Monty Python, something completely different. But no. Get this – not only did Dave stay and fight for his place but he eventually usurped Eric, was called upon to represent Wales at under-23 level, joined Newcastle United in a big-money transfer and subsequently assumed the mantle of Welsh first-team goalkeeper, making his full international debut against Brazil and rooming with the great John Charles on away trips. Talk about redemption.

Anyway, back to my interview with Eric who, at the time we initially spoke, was a sprightly 89, living in the picturesque Sussex coastal town of Peacehaven. There we were, chatting away over the phone, and it's all fascinating stuff – playing in the 50s and 60s, becoming a minor celebrity, life after football, and so on. I mentioned Dave Hollins in passing and Eric spoke warmly of his former understudy and rival. Then, in a throwaway remark that very nearly escaped me, Eric let slip that they were still friends.

The journalist in me, sensing something out of left field, probed further. This, it emerged, was anything but the kind of friendship where people just send each other a Christmas card and that's about it. These two octogenarians had, at least until Covid arrived, met up every few weeks to chew the fat over a milky brew, lunch or a game of bowls. Actually, I take that back. Bowls, I now appreciate, is serious stuff and something that continues to satisfy both men's competitive urges, not a chew-the-fat kind of activity. Sixty-five years after football had first thrown them together, they were still thick as thieves.

Now, this struck me as truly astonishing, for three reasons.

One. Footballers aren't very good at keeping in touch with each other. They're not so much ships that pass in the night, more like ships that put into port and spend time berthed alongside each other before scattering to all points of the compass. Eventually they retire. Sure, there are reunion dinners for the more successful teams, while some clubs preside over former players' associations that organise occasional events. However, the hard yards behind such affairs tend to be put in by people who remember those players fondly, rather than the actual players themselves. The sad truth is that when a player leaves a club, they're unlikely to speak to the majority of their ex-team-mates again.

Two. Eric and Dave were rivals. Although it's often said there's an unofficial union among goalkeepers, formed in the knowledge that one mistake on their part can lose a match or, at worst, end careers, this empathy doesn't always extend to keepers at the same club. It certainly didn't in the 1950s when players in the first team automatically received a better wage than those in the reserves. With bills to pay and a woman's place still deemed to be largely in the home, unable to contribute financially to the running of the household, resentment could easily brew. Then there was the retained list, drawn up by managers at the end of every season. If you weren't in the first XI there was every possibility you might not make the list and, consequently, would be seeking employment elsewhere come May. In such circumstances, you can hardly blame footballers for being, to quote Eric, 'For myself and nobody else.'

Three. I've written about sport for many years and I'd never come across a genuine friendship between former team-mates or opponents that had lasted so long. This was different to, say, long-retired former tennis players I knew who renewed acquaintances once a year over a bottle of red in the private restaurants of Wimbledon. Dave had known Eric longer than he'd known his wife Jackie (putting that into context, Dave and Jackie first met in April 1957). They were the kind of natural pals who didn't need an occasion to bring them together. I spoke to several of my peers in the sports press fraternity and they couldn't think of anything like it either. As far as I and seemingly everybody else could work out, theirs appeared to be the firmest, most enduring friendship in elite British sport.

I wrote my article about Eric. Three months later, having been given Dave's telephone number by Eric, I also interviewed and wrote an article about Dave. Both pieces attracted much warmth and attention.

... which helped fan the flames of what came next.

As a journalist, very, very occasionally you'll come across a story that deserves far more space than you've been assigned by an editor. A book, in other words. This was one of those rare occasions. Individually, their stories were fascinating. Together, they went to another level.

Then there was the timing. Eric and Dave weren't getting any younger. Heck, none of us are. When we go, we risk taking our stories with us. That, so I find, is increasingly the case with sportsmen and women whose heydays preceded the digital revolution. We've become so obsessed with the here and now, documenting sporting careers and events that are still unfolding, that we're in danger of allowing the past to escape us. So much of what went reported prior to the 21st century became fish and chip paper or was wiped by those who failed to recognise its historical significance. Bits and pieces may still exist in libraries or museums but, by and large, once it's gone, it's gone. And that's before you stop to consider all the things that didn't get reported in the first place.

Here were two men, their lives bookended by the extremes of the Second World War and the Covid-19 pandemic, whose football careers spanned a time that's been grossly under-represented in sports literature. When Eric and Dave first pulled on their string goalkeeping gloves there really was, as the Clash once sang, 'no Elvis, Beatles or The Rolling Stones'. Transatlantic travel, in all probability, meant by boat. Trains were uniformly hauled by steam engines. John F. Kennedy was barely known outside Massachusetts. Dementia was a grisly 1955 horror film set in downtown Los Angeles, not something that came with heading footballs.

In short, Eric and Dave had remarkable stories to tell from across eight different decades (ten if you include the 1930s and 1940s before football brought them together). If they didn't get told now, then they probably never would.

I asked the two of them whether they'd be up for being the subjects of a book, and they both said yes. I asked a publisher, unquestionably the best right now at telling the kind of disparate sports stories that never used to be told, if they'd be up for releasing it. They said yes as well.

... and here we are.

Spencer Vignes
Cardiff, Wales
July 2022

1

WE'LL MEET AGAIN

'Not liking the look of this.' – Helen Branswell,
science journalist specialising in infectious
diseases, 2 January 2020

IT'S WEDNESDAY, 12 February 2020. Britain is 40 days away from being locked down in a bid to combat the effects of the Covid-19 pandemic. At present, the majority of new cases being reported are inside China. But the situation is changing by the minute. It takes just one international air flight to transport the virus to the opposite side of the globe. Today, the skies pretty much everywhere are full of commercial airliners. It's Hollywood disaster movie stuff with cherries on top.

And yet, at Denton Island Indoor Bowls Club in the English port town of Newhaven, none of that matters right now. Why? Because it's time to play bowls.

Denton Island's team for this morning's inter-club match consists of three people. Playing lead and second, step forward Eric Gill and Dave Hollins, respectively, two men accustomed to performing inside some of the most famous sporting arenas in the world, albeit as association football goalkeepers rather than bowlers.

Between 1951 and 1970, Eric and Dave ran out in front of many millions – yes, *millions* – of spectators packed inside stadiums such as Old Trafford, Anfield, Hampden Park and Rio's Maracanã to pit their wits against the likes of Stanley Matthews, George Best, Jimmy Greaves, Pelé, Garrincha, Vavá, Denis Law, Jack Rowley, Tom Finney and Bobby Charlton, not to mention their shared nemesis, Brian Clough. They didn't always come out on top – we're talking some of the finest attacking talent ever to set foot on a football field here – but they gave their level best on every occasion. As Dave himself admits, 'When you share the same blades of grass with people like that, it's an honour. You can only admire high skill.'

Of course, it wasn't always that glamorous. There were also Tuesday nights in January away to Torquay United and Barrow and Swansea Town, guarding goalmouths peppered with flint against journeymen centre-forwards hell-bent on sending them to the nearest infirmary at the earliest opportunity. But then the idea, dear reader, is to try to 'sell' you this book in the early pages, not to put you off. We'll get to the warts and all in due course. For the time being, let's give the pearls top billing.

Today, there's no crowd at Denton Island. There rarely is at inter-club bowls matches. Yet, as far as Eric and Dave are concerned, the discipline remains the same as it did throughout all those afternoons and evenings spent guarding goalmouths in far-off towns and cities – absolute concentration.

'You get to meet a lot of great friends playing bowls,' says Eric, north London accent still resolutely intact. 'It's a very social game. But it's also very competitive. Don't let anybody tell you otherwise. And I've always been competitive. Gotta win, that's me. Gotta win.'

With that, Eric adopts his game face, takes hold of the first of his woods (bowling parlance for the actual bowls), eyes the yellow jack at the far end of the rink, and goes to work.

Fast forward 23 months …

With hindsight, Covid must have been much closer that morning than either Eric or Dave realised. The clues were there in plain sight: only one person allowed to touch the jack; only one person allowed to touch the mat; chairs arranged six feet apart for players to sit on while changing their shoes; face masks to be worn right up until the point of bowling (although Dave, asthmatic since childhood, remained exempt). All just precautionary measures, nothing serious, you understand.

How little they, we, knew.

As for the identity of the opposing team and the result? Neither Eric, Dave nor Irene Taylor, Eric's partner in real life and the third member of the team that day, can remember. All three have excellent memories but the events of 2020, 2021 and 2022 have simply sheared what's important in the mind from what isn't. Bowling is a serious business, but it's not that serious.

The one thing they're all agreed on is this: it was the last time any of them went bowling for a long, long time. It was also the last occasion that Eric and Dave, close friends since the days when Marilyn Monroe was just plain old Norma Jeane Mortenson, saw each other face to face for almost two years.

The first of England's lockdowns, when it finally came on 23 March 2020, had brought with it a terrible sense of foreboding for Dave bordering on déjà vu. In 2017 his brother, John Hollins, himself a former professional footballer, returned from a pre-season tour of China by Arsenal, one of his ex-clubs, with a peculiar virus. Within days all his main organs had shut down. John was kept alive by doctors at the Chelsea and Westminster Hospital in London, where he remained in intensive care for three weeks. The road to recovery was a long one but he survived. Just.

Dave had no idea whether this new virus was what had befallen his brother. Probably not, considering Covid-19 wasn't officially identified until two years later in the December of 2019. All he knew was it came from the same part of the world and the symptoms were remarkably similar. That was enough to scare the bejesus out of him and take all the health warnings seriously. To hell with the Covid deniers – the drawbridge to this English born and raised Welsh international's castle was going up for the foreseeable future.

Over the weeks and months that followed, many leaders, heads of state, commentators and journalists fell back on wartime metaphors to describe the challenges mankind was facing. Doctors and nurses became soldiers. People breaking social-distancing rules became traitors or deserters. 'We will meet again,' declared Queen Elizabeth

II in a broadcast to the UK and Commonwealth on 5 April 2020, drawing on the 1939 song made famous by Vera Lynn to evoke the Blitz spirit of the Second World War.

It was a language both Eric and Dave were only too familiar with, having survived some of the worst of what the Second World War had to offer. But they were words that also stood them in good stead. On that occasion Eric and Dave had come through the mire as children. This time they were determined to come through it again as old men.

2

A MATTER OF LIFE AND DEATH

*'This morning the British ambassador in Berlin
handed the German government a final note,
stating that unless we heard from them, by
11 o'clock, that they were prepared at once to
withdraw their troops from Poland, a state of
war would exist between us. I have to tell you
now that no such undertaking has been received
and that, consequently, this country is at war
with Germany.'* – Neville Chamberlain

THE PARACHUTE mine drifted down out of the night
sky and came to rest a few yards from the front door of
17 Swinley House, Redhill Street, London NW1, home
of the Gill family. Twenty-five seconds after making
contact with the ground, parachute mines were primed
to detonate, laying waste to anything in their immediate
vicinity.

... except that this one didn't detonate.

If it had, then the Swinley House flats, along quite
probably with the majority of its occupants, would have

been history. Curtains for Eric Gill at the tender age of 11. Forget about the outstanding goalkeeping career and everything else to come. You, dear reader, would now be doing something else with your time. On such sliding door moments do our lives depend.

And here's the punchline – a second parachute mine fell that very same night on the church adjacent to Swinley House, coming to rest wrapped around its steeple. That didn't detonate either. Small wonder Eric has always considered himself to be lucky.

Swinley House had been a big step up in the world for the Gill family. Home until early 1932 for John and Emily along with their three sons, William, Jack and Eric, had been 60 Augustus Street, a slum area to the east of London's Regent's Park built on land owned by the Crown Estate. Within months of Eric being born on 3 November 1930, it was announced that the Augustus Street properties were to be condemned. Cue the move to Swinley House.

'Moving into that flat was like moving into a palace for us,' remembers Eric. 'It was a brand-new flat with an inside toilet, something we'd never had before. In the old place, the toilet had been out in the yard. When my mum and dad first got married, all they'd been able to afford to rent was one room in a slum house on a slum street. The minute I was born, along comes this new flat. That's why I always tell people I was born lucky.'

It was, at least until the bombs and parachute mines started to fall, an idyllic childhood. Swinley House backed on to a spur off the Regent's Canal which, in turn, fed into the busier Grand Union Canal linking England's capital with its second city of Birmingham. From the window Eric would sit and watch the barges pass, hazarding guesses at what lay beneath in their cargo holds. When he'd had enough of that, Regent's Park, with its enticing blend of wide-open spaces and leafy hideaways, beckoned. And when he'd tired of that, there was always football.

'Looking back, I think most of my time was spent out playing football with my mates,' says Eric. 'We'd use the streets because there wasn't many cars back then. We had this spot where there was a gentlemen's toilets and the front of that was our goal. Nobody had an actual football, so we'd use a tennis ball instead. They were all local lads, most of who lived in the same flats and went to the same school, Netley Primary, as me. I can't remember who used to go in goal but it certainly wasn't me. I was always playing out. It wasn't until I was 14, possibly even 15, that I started getting a thing for going in goal.'

On 3 September 1939, a couple of months before Eric turned nine years old, Britain and France declared war on Germany in response to Adolf Hitler's decision to invade Poland. *Auf Wiedersehen* to the idyllic childhood. Initially Eric was evacuated to the Buckinghamshire village of Stokenchurch to live with an aunt. However, for a young Londoner the peace and quiet of the countryside was deafening, not to mention dull beyond belief. Eric begged his parents to come and take him home. Which they did.

For the next six years, Eric saw out the war at the epicentre of one of Hitler's principal targets. Once the so-called 'Phoney War' spanning September 1939 to May 1940 was over, so the battering of London began. On several occasions firewatchers extinguished incendiary bombs that landed on the roof of the Swinley House flats (living lower down on the first floor, the Gills felt a degree of protection from these). Another bomb blew out the majority of the windows in the block, including all those belonging to number 17. Then there were the two faulty parachute mines. Lucky? You betcha.

Unfortunately, that luck didn't quite extend to everyone in the Gill family. William Gill, eldest of the three Gill boys, had been 18 when the Second World War broke out. He joined the Royal Marines as a regular and, as of 18 March 1941, became part of HMS *Dunedin*'s company. Launched in 1918 and originally part of the Royal Navy's New Zealand Division, *Dunedin* had returned from the South Pacific in 1937 and, throughout the majority of 1941, spent its time patrolling the South Atlantic following up on intelligence gleaned largely from Enigma code breakers based at Bletchley Park in Buckinghamshire.

On 24 November, the light cruiser was steaming on a north-west course approximately 900 miles west of the Sierra Leone port of Freetown when it was sighted by a German U-boat. Although *Dunedin*'s lookout spotted the submarine's periscope, enabling the ship to take evasive action, the U-boat's captain, Jochen Mohr, nevertheless chose to try his luck by firing three torpedoes from a speculative distance of 4,000 yards. Incredibly two of them found their mark. Within 17 minutes of being hit, *Dunedin* had turned on its beam-ends and sunk.

'It had been in the paper that the ship had been torpedoed and gone down,' Eric recalls. 'We didn't know anything else. Then one day we received the telegram. It said, "Reported missing, presumed dead". It was a terrible, terrible thing. You don't forget days like that in a hurry. I don't know if we were expecting the worst by then or still holding out for the best. And that seemed to be that.'

What happened next only really became apparent many years later through extensive research by members of the HMS Dunedin Society. Around 250 men went into the water from the ship's complement of nearly 500. Over the following three days their numbers dwindled due to a combination of heat, insanity, sharks and drowning. *Dunedin* had gone down in the early afternoon just south of the equator. Many of the crew were wearing shorts at the time. Cast adrift, they had little in the way of clothing to protect them from the scorching heat of the day and the chill brought on by night.

In the late afternoon of 27 November, a US merchant ship, *Nishmaha*, heading from Takoradi in Ghana to Philadelphia, happened to stumble across the 72 remaining survivors spread out across six life rafts. William, or Bill as he was better known among friends and shipmates, was one of only three men still alive in the first raft to be recovered. By the time the ship docked in Trinidad, a further five men had died, bringing the survivor total down to just 67.

Over the next few weeks, the 67 were nursed back to some semblance of health thanks to a combination of the Trinidadian health service and local families who rallied to take the men in. Bill finally returned to England in January 1942. He went on to marry, having three children and seven grandchildren, and became founding president of the HMS Dunedin Society, living to the age of 92.

'Our mother was a lovely lady, gave herself to the family, but she was such a worrier, and I really don't think what William went through helped,' Eric reflects. 'She had three sons and she spent her life looking after them, worrying herself sick about us. She was such a worrier that she never, ever saw me play football in all my 20 years as a professional. She once said to me, "I'm sorry but I can't come, I'm frightened you'll get injured." It wasn't that she didn't care. It was nerves. If she was like that with football, you can imagine what she was like with one son reported missing presumed dead.'

* * *

Approximately 30 miles south-west of London, nestling in a valley amid the North Downs on the banks of the River Wey, lies Guildford, a bustling market town which despite having a cathedral isn't, in fact, a city. Nice shops, clean air, some of the priciest real estate in the UK, pretty much everything back in 1939 that London NW1 wasn't. War, however, has a habit of being a great leveller.

It was here that Bill Hollins, once the last line of defence for Wolverhampton Wanderers, brought his young family when the curtain came down on his career as a professional goalkeeper. Bill's wife, Joanna, was from Guildford and had sisters aplenty there – always handy when it comes to ready-made childminders. The couple would eventually have five children, four boys and a girl. There was Roy, Dave, Maureen, Tony and John. Roy, Dave and John would all go on to become professional footballers in their own right. That didn't tend to happen in the stockbroker factory that was, and indeed remains, Guildford.

Unlike London, Guildford wasn't exactly high up on Hitler's list of key objectives. And yet, in common with so many provincial outposts, it soon found itself drawn into the theatre of war. In late May and early June of 1940, the town's railway station became a hub for the Dunkirk evacuation as train upon train ferried thousands of bedraggled troops away from the south coast ports in search of clothing, sustenance and medical attention. Before long the drone of Allied and Axis aircraft heading south and north to attack their respective targets ranked second only on the Guildford breeze to birdsong. Occasionally, that distant drone grew altogether louder into something far more menacing.

'One afternoon my elder brother and I were playing in the back garden and this plane, a German one, came over low and started firing its guns,' says Dave. 'All of a sudden, my Auntie Kath came running out, grabbed hold of the two of us and pulled us inside to safety. I think he was getting rid of all his bullets before flying out over the English Channel back to wherever he'd come from. That was pretty hairy. Well, it was more than that, I realise now. I think we were pretty near to death there.'

In December 1942, in a remarkably similar incident a couple of miles away in the village of Bramley, another lone bomber, which had strayed from its formation, attacked a train that had just set off from Guildford. Eight of the 20 passengers on board were killed, while the remaining 12 all suffered injuries of some kind. Only the steam engine's fireman escaped unharmed to tend to the dying and wounded, with both the driver and guard also perishing in the ambush.

As the tide turned in favour of Britain and its Allies, so Germany began to unleash its 'vengeance weapons', flying bombs in the shape of rockets fired from launch pads in north-east France towards south-east England. There were the devastating V2s that flew so fast you never heard them coming. They just arrived with a colossal, and often deadly, bang.

Worse still, in Dave's opinion, were the V1s, nicknamed doodlebugs or buzz bombs. 'They made a noise like the loudest truck you've ever heard struggling to climb a hill,' he recalls. 'When they ran out of fuel, the noise would stop and they would fall to earth on top of anyone or anything unfortunate enough to be directly beneath it. One of my best friends who lived at the top of our road went out for the day and came home to find his house completely destroyed. Those few seconds between the noise cutting out and the buzz bomb landing were terrifying. There's no other word for it. All you could do was hold your breath and hope.'

Today, many professional goalkeepers make use of sports psychologists in an attempt not only to improve their all-round performance but also to recover from mistakes or setbacks – spilling a tame shot over the goal line, giving away a soft penalty, dealing with abuse from supporters, reading criticism in the media – you get the picture. In the 1950s and 1960s what constituted player welfare was, it's fair to say, more primitive to the point of being non-existent. Then again, having bombs and rockets fall around you on a regular basis, believing your brother to be dead in the Atlantic and being strafed while playing in the back garden are the sort of formative experiences that tend to come hand in hand with a healthy sense of perspective in adult life. No doubt about it, keeping the ball out of the net was a serious business. However, if you made a mistake, then so be it. Move on. It wasn't the end of the world. Eric knew that. Dave knew that. And so did the vast majority of their post-war goalkeeping peers.

* * *

Eric and Dave were 14 and 7 years old, respectively, when the war finally ended in 1945. Academically, Dave still had plenty of time to claw back what remained of his state education. Not so Eric, who'd missed large chunks of his schooling due to the fact that the school in question was, more often than not, closed due to the effects of the bombing, or at best open half-days only.

'My father said to me, "Look, you're not very good with a pen and paper because you've lost most of your education. I suggest you get a job where you're perhaps working in a factory. What about getting an apprenticeship as a toolmaker?" So that's what I did. I got a job working in a big factory on the Holloway Road in north London. But I hated it. There was no natural light and with them machines going all the time it was so noisy. It wasn't for me and I didn't stay very long.'

Next, Eric got a job as a printer. That wasn't for him either. Ditto the briefest of stints as a sheet metal worker.

'In the end my father said, "I think you'd better come and work with me." He worked as a brass finisher in a factory called Galsworthy Limited, which did a bit of all sorts to do with brass and tools and metals. He was a very intelligent guy, my father, someone who should've perhaps done more for himself in life but was quite happy where he was. It was only a small factory but important enough to make stuff for the war effort, which is why my father stayed at home instead of going away to fight. During the war, somebody from the government came down and told everybody in the factory to do one particular job, and they did that and nothing else. My father was put to work making the mechanism that released the harness when pilots ejected from their planes. That's what I did as well when I went to work there, because the war still hadn't quite finished at that point. I loved that place, I really did, and I got on with everybody there, helped no doubt by the fact that everybody got on with my father.'

At some point not long after hostilities ceased, John Gill took his youngest son to watch Chelsea in action. As the match wore on, so Eric found his attention drawn towards the figure guarding Chelsea's goal. Vic Woodley was, by that time, in the twilight of a career that had yielded 19 England caps and over 250 first-team appearances for the Blues. If his powers as a goalkeeper were waning, then Eric certainly wasn't aware of it.

'That was the first professional football match I ever saw, Chelsea versus whoever they were playing against, and there he was, Vic Woodley,' Eric recalls. 'I was amazed. Whenever anyone took a shot at goal, he always got himself behind the ball. I didn't know how he did it but, watching him that day, he became my hero. I thought, *God almighty, I wish I could play like that*! A lot of goalkeepers say they were born to play in that position. Well that certainly wasn't me. I'd been playing centre-half until then, having started my own team in Regent's Park. We had another kid who'd gone in goal and he was quite good. But once I'd seen Vic Woodley, something changed. I wanted to be him.'

And so Eric started playing in goal for a club called Broomfield based in the north London suburb of Palmers Green. It just so happened that Broomfield's president was Joe Hulme, manager of Tottenham Hotspur. On a tip-off, Hulme made a point of watching Eric in action before telling the teenage rookie, 'I'll come for you when I'm ready.'

Eric waited, and waited some more, but Hulme never came. Far from being downhearted, Eric decided that if Tottenham didn't want him as a goalkeeper, maybe someone else might.

'I wasn't the best at writing, so I asked my father if he'd write some letters on my behalf, which we could send to a few professional clubs,' Eric recollects. 'We wrote to Arsenal, Chelsea and Charlton, enclosing stamped addressed envelopes, asking for trials. Chelsea wrote back saying they weren't holding any trials. Arsenal didn't even bother replying. And Charlton wrote back saying, "Bring your boots on Saturday." That's how it all started. I didn't even know where Charlton was! I had to find out how to get there and, when I came out of the train station, ask someone the way to the ground. It's not far – you come out of the station, over the bridge and walk down the road – but I didn't know that.'

Eric played well enough in his trial match that Saturday for Charlton Athletic to offer him a professional contract on £6 per week with a £10 signing-on fee, no mean feat for a 17-year-old who'd only been playing in goal for a couple of years.

'I was pleased as punch,' he declares. 'I said "Oh yeah, where's the paper, give me the pen!" They said, "Hold on, it doesn't quite work like that. We've got to come and see your mother and father first." So, Bob Wright, who was assistant to Jimmy Seed, Charlton's manager, came up to the flat in Camden and spoke to my mum and dad, saying all the things they say to try and put parents off. You know, "Only one in 200 players that we sign make it into the first team and become professionals," and what have you. I said, "I don't care, I still want to sign." He said, "Well, it's up to your mum and dad." Thankfully, they said I could.'

The half-a-dozen or so years that followed the Second World War were bumper times for British football. Starved of entertainment throughout the hostilities, hundreds of thousands of demobbed men with gratuities to burn made for their local clubs once regular fixtures resumed. The 1946/47 season saw attendance figures for Football League matches hit a record 35 million spectators, rising to in excess of 40 million for each of the three campaigns spanning 1947/48 to 1949/50. At a time of austerity, mourning, rationing and drabness, football's golden years, as they became known, did more perhaps than anything else to raise morale from Arbroath to Exeter.

Riding the crest of this social and sporting renaissance were Charlton Athletic. They reached the FA Cup Final in 1946, losing to Derby County. They reached the FA Cup Final again in 1947, beating Burnley. They boasted one of the largest league grounds in the UK, often drawing crowds in excess of 70,000 to The Valley. They didn't always set English football's First Division (the equivalent of today's Premier League) alight in terms of their league form, but at least they were up there dining at the high table.

Into this vast cauldron of south-east London life during the spring of 1948 walked Eric. Most professional football clubs back then had three teams – the first team, the reserves (which in Charlton's case competed in the Football Combination, a league for second XIs from across mainly southern England) and an 'A' team, or the thirds. Eric, so he was told, was to cut his teeth keeping goal for the 'A' team. If he excelled, there was every chance he'd progress through the ranks.

A 17-year-old, signed by a top-flight football club barely two years after first deciding to take up goalkeeping, with nothing in the way of specialist coaching behind him. Wouldn't happen now, what with academies and pathways and what have you. Not a chance. Which is bad news for life's late developers, if you can call 17 late.

Mind you, whatever joy Eric felt at trading the factory floor for the football field was tempered by two things. The first went by the name of Sam Bartram. Widely reckoned to be the finest goalkeeper never to play for England, County Durham-born Bartram was slap bang in the middle of creating a new (and still existing) appearance record for Charlton of 623 league and cup matches, something that would keep him busy until the age of 42. To Eric, the man seemed immovable. And, ultimately, so he'd prove to be. But let's not get ahead of ourselves. For the time being at least, Eric was simply glad to be third in line at the party.

The second obstacle came in the form of National Service. The end of the Second World War didn't mean an end to British military commitments abroad. There was an empire, albeit diminishing, to oversee, post-war occupation commitments in Germany and Japan, plus a desire to re-establish influence in various parts of the world, including the Middle East, not to mention escalating events in the Cold War outpost of Korea and India post-independence. To meet such challenges, a standardised form of peacetime conscription was introduced in 1947 for all able-bodied British men between the ages of 18 and 30. Initially, each man was to serve for 18 months. However, the outbreak of war in Korea in 1950 saw this increased to two years.

For footballers and indeed all elite male sportsmen, National Service represented a somewhat hazardous crossroads. Turn one way and your career could effectively be over, courtesy of anything from instantaneous death to wear and tear on the body. Turn the other and, if you were fortunate enough to be befriended by some kind of guardian angel with a military rank, there was every likelihood you'd be nursed through your National Service in relative comfort. When Eric's papers arrived late in 1948, Lady Luck once again stepped in to guide him down the latter path.

'Before I was called up, I was asked to go and see Jimmy Seed in his office at Charlton, and there sitting next to him was a military man, a captain,' Eric recalls. 'He said to me, "I'm Captain so and so. When you get called up, you're to be posted to Hilsea Barracks in Portsmouth and you'll play football for the Royal Army Ordnance Corps. We've never won the Army Cup and we're determined to get that on our CV." Then he said, "When you receive your papers, it'll tell you to register at your local labour exchange in Camden … but I don't want you to do that. I want you to go to Deptford instead." I said I didn't understand but he said, "You don't have to understand. Just do as I tell you – go to Deptford, not Camden."

'Anyway, a few weeks later when I got my papers I went down to Deptford as I'd been told by this captain. Someone came up to me, asked who I was, and I said, "Eric Gill." Straight off they went, "We've been waiting for you!" They took me round the back, avoiding all the queues, sat me down, took my particulars and said, "You're going to Parsons Barracks in Aldershot for two weeks where you'll get your rifle, clothes and stuff, then you'll go to Hilsea Barracks in Portsmouth until you're demobbed." It was unbelievable. They said, "You're going there to play football – that's it." That sounded good to me! I didn't know how this ruse or whatever it was worked. I just decided that I was going to do what I was told.'

So, Eric made his way to Hilsea Barracks via Aldershot to join up with the Royal Army Ordnance Corps, where he soon discovered 'this ruse or whatever it was' made professional footballers something of a target for professional military men.

'We got a lot of privileges and, because of that, there were certain people who didn't like us. We had one major in the company who absolutely hated footballers and would do his best to get us into trouble. But try as he might, he never succeeded. He put me on a charge once and I was marched in front of the powers that be for this charge to be read out. It was for something like failing to salute a military car with an officer inside while it was flying a flag, something you were supposed to do. Apparently, I'd walked right past without acknowledging it. This major, he thought, *At last! I've got a footballer.* But it got thrown out straight away. Whoever was presiding just said, "For God's sake, get him out of here!" And off I went.'

Eric might not have been much of a soldier – through no fault of his own, mind – but he served his purpose at Hilsea. In between returning to Charlton on leave to play the occasional match for the 'A' team or reserves, Eric took his place between the posts as the Royal Army Ordnance Corps set about capturing the prestigious Army Cup. On 10 April 1950 their team of assembled Football League all-stars beat the Royal Artillery's team of assembled Football League all-stars 2-1 in the final at Aldershot in front of King George VI and Queen Elizabeth, the future Queen Mother.

'We had a good side, including John Cumming of Hearts and Jackie Henderson of Portsmouth, but then they had some handy players of their own, like Ivor Allchurch, one of the future greats of Welsh football, so it was always going to be a hard game,' says Eric. 'We were introduced to the King before the match and then to him and the Queen after the final whistle when it came to receiving the cup and our medals. He was quite ill at the time. In fact, it was only a year or two before he died. He had a suit on, which had batteries in the pocket that were all wired up to help keep him warm. She spoke to me, which was a great honour, but he didn't speak at all. He was there though – that was the main thing. He done his duty.'

Once his National Service was over, Eric returned full-time to Charlton and life in the shadow of Sam Bartram, melded as ever to the first-team goalkeeper's jersey. No matter how well Eric or any of the other goalkeepers on Charlton's books played for the reserves or 'A' team, as long as Bartram maintained his high standards and fitness, they were simply never going to get a look-in.

'Sam was wonderful, a lovely guy, he really was, always happy to give me a helping hand or some advice,' Eric admits. 'But he was the number one for something like 20 years. That meant a lot of goalkeepers – and we did have a lot of goalkeepers at Charlton – didn't get much of an opportunity. When we had practice matches, I often used to play out on the field to keep myself entertained. We had one match [for the 'A' team against Bexleyheath & Welling in the semi-final of the Woolwich Memorial Hospital Cup] when Jimmy Seed decided to play me as a centre-forward ... and I scored a goal! I didn't feel out of my depth at all. In fact, I felt quite at home playing there. But I was never going to give up being a goalkeeper, even with Sam around. It was just a case of waiting to see if a chance would ever come along.'

On Wednesday, 5 September 1951, Eric's patience was finally rewarded when Bartram was declared unfit for Charlton's First Division fixture against Manchester United. Rather than selecting the South African-born keeper Albert Uytenbogaardt, the other chief potential beneficiary of Bartram's misfortune, Jimmy Seed opted instead to hand Eric his first-team debut. At Old Trafford, of all places.

The Manchester United of 1951 wasn't the Manchester United of Alex Ferguson, or Bryan Robson, or George Best, or even Duncan Edwards. The Munich air disaster was still seven years away – that's how long ago we're talking about here. But it was the Manchester United of Matt Busby who, having taken over the managerial reins in 1945, had set about assembling the first of several great teams, one that would win the FA Cup in 1948 and finish runners-up in the First Division in 1947, 1948, 1949 and 1951, before finally winning it in 1952. Old Trafford already had an aura, in other words.

Spearheading United's frontline throughout those years was Wolverhampton-born Jack Rowley, one of only four players ever to have notched over 200 goals for the club (the others being Bobby Charlton, Denis Law and Wayne Rooney). Nicknamed 'The Gunner' for his prolific scoring rate and explosive shooting, Rowley wasn't the sort of striker that a goalkeeper particularly wanted to come across on their full debut. Still, in at the deep end, as they say.

'In them days goalkeepers didn't get protection,' says Eric. 'I could go up and catch the ball in mid-air and a forward would come in at speed and barge me over. You might have seen that footage of Nat Lofthouse smashing Harry Gregg, Manchester United's goalkeeper, into his net in the 1958 FA Cup Final. Well, that kind of stuff used to happen all the time. Anyway, Jack Rowley, he comes charging in when I'm up in the air. I catch the ball and he knocks me flying into the goal with the ball ... and the referee gave the goal! That would never happen these days but, as I said, it was a wee bit different then. That was how football was played. You had to learn to stand up or get out of the way.'

Charlton lost the match 3-2 having led 2-1 until the 87th minute but Eric played well enough for a section of the Manchester United crowd to applaud him as he left the field, a gesture he's never forgotten. Alas, no matter how well he'd performed, that didn't prevent Jimmy Seed from restoring the fit-again Sam Bartram to first-team duty against Middlesbrough three days later. Not that Eric harboured any resentment at the decision. If anything, the Manchester United match served as a reminder of how much he still had to learn, particularly when it came to dealing with battle-hardened centre-forwards like Jack Rowley.

'That match more than any other taught me that when you went up to catch a ball, you had to put your feet up and bring your knees up high,' adds Eric. 'That way, if a player came charging in at me, I had a sort of protective shield. Centre-forwards, they didn't like that. They just wanted to rush in and barge you full in the chest. So, I set about learning how to catch the ball with my knees up. That way, if they did come at you, then there was every chance they would come off worse than you.'

The 3-2 defeat at Old Trafford proved to be Eric's one and only appearance for Charlton's first team during four National Service-interrupted years at the club. His final match prior to being placed on the transfer list with a price tag of £400 came in an 'A' team fixture against Fulham on 20 March 1952. By that time Eric had already decided that his future lay somewhere other than The Valley, largely as a result of a conversation he'd had with Sam Bartram.

'Sam said to me, "I'm sorry, but you'd be much better off if you left this club and found yourself another one where you can play first-team football." He said, "There's no openings for you here. Have a look around and see what you can find. Don't let your career pass you by." He was like that, Sam. He really did care. So, I decided to take his advice. A couple of clubs came after me. One was Torquay United and the other Bristol Rovers. Their assistant manager was Bob Wright, who'd been assistant to Jimmy Seed when I first joined Charlton. He asked me to go down to Bristol and have a chat with him, which I did. He said, "Right, we'd like to sign you, but you're being paid by Charlton up until the end of July [1952], so we don't want to sign you just yet. They might as well keep paying you for the time being." Then he says, "I'm coming up to Lord's to see the Test match around then. You don't live far from Lord's. I'll watch the Test match, then come over to your house and sign you." I was still living in Swinley House with my parents at the time. So, I said fine and we left it at that.'

Big mistake, at least on the part of Bristol Rovers. Two years previously a man by the name of Billy Lane, poised to become manager of Brighton & Hove Albion, had watched Eric play in the quarter-final of the Army Cup for the Royal Army Ordnance Corps against the Royal Army Medical Corps. Lane was impressed enough with Eric's performance that day to put a star by his name in the notebook that accompanied him on all scouting missions, a reminder that here was someone worth keeping tabs on.

Now word reached Lane via football's bush telegraph that Eric was available and seeking a new challenge. The only fly in the ointment was Bristol Rovers. However, Eric still hadn't put pen to paper on any deal with the west country club. If he was going to get his man, then Lane had to act swiftly.

'This telegram turned up from Billy Lane, manager of Brighton, saying, "Catch the 10am train to Brighton and I'll meet you at the station,"' Eric recalls. 'I thought, *Oh my God! Well, I'll go just to see what's happening.* I'd never been to Brighton before in my life. I knew it was a holiday resort but that was about all. So, I caught the train down, met Billy Lane at the station, and he took me to a very posh restaurant for a meal. Afterwards we went to the ground, which was the old Goldstone Ground in them days, and he said, "Right, I want to sign you, put your name on this contract." He wanted the deal done there and then, probably to stop Bristol Rovers from getting hold of me. And I was quite happy about that. So, I signed. I don't think Bristol Rovers were too pleased. He [Bob Wright] didn't come to our house anyway. I never saw him again.'

On signing the contract, Brighton paid Charlton the £400 asking fee (worth about £12,000 in 2022 prices), which, in a remarkable act of generosity, Charlton then gave straight to Eric as 'accrued benefits' (pay that an employee has earned based on their service, due at a later date) in recognition of his conscientiousness while understudying Sam Bartram, in effect setting him up to start a new life in Brighton.

'They were pretty good at looking after their players,' maintains Eric of the club that gave him his big break in the game. 'But Sam was right – I had to get away from

Charlton. In the event, leaving was the best thing that ever happened to me.'

With that, so the opening chapter of Eric Gill's goalkeeping career came to a close. For Dave Hollins, however, the introduction was only just being written.

3

THE THIRD WAY

'Grab it while you can – grab every scrap of
happiness while you can.' – Noël Coward

A ROAD to Damascus moment at a Chelsea match as a 15-year-old followed by an explosion of raw talent that took him from Broomfield to Brighton & Hove Albion via Charlton Athletic and the army. That was Eric.

For Dave, however, the journey couldn't have been more different.

'I suppose you could say that goalkeeping was quite literally in my blood,' Dave admits. 'Dad was a Midlands lad who'd played in goal for Stoke and then Wolves when Stan Cullis was their manager. When I was 15, he thought I was ready for some intermediate football, so he took me along to Merrow, an amateur club on the outskirts of Guildford where my older brother Roy also played. It was quite a good standard of football. Dad would stand behind the goal and coach me during games and I'd invariably end up in the back of the net, with the ball in my hands, because I was competing against men, and football in those days was highly physical. He'd say, "Get up son, come on, get up," and I'd get up, catch the next cross that came my way and try and forget about the last cross I'd caught and how I'd been knocked flying into the net by some colossal striker twice my age.'

Guildford and London NW1 may have been poles apart in terms of their social and economic DNA, but that's not to say Dave's childhood differed markedly from Eric's. With five young mouths to cater for, money not to mention food could be scarce in the Hollins household. Dad Bill did his level best to make ends meet by holding down two jobs, unloading milk churns during the day for the Co-op before heading across town to St Luke's Hospital to perform his nocturnal duties as an orderly. Quite how he managed it given the state of his fingers, so badly gnarled by the effects of saving heavy leather footballs that he'd been prevented from serving in the Second World War, was anyone's guess. But he did.

Prior to Merrow, Dave's world had revolved around Stoughton Recreation Ground and the impromptu 22-a-side football matches that would break out between local children. Another slightly older boy by the name of Ray Drinkwater had cut his goalkeeping teeth playing in the same free-for-alls before the ambitious semi-professional club Guildford City signed him. Dave grew to idolise Ray who, despite his somewhat tough, rebellious streak, graduated to stand between the posts for Portsmouth and Queens Park Rangers.

'I used to think, *In no way will I have the same attitude as him*,' Dave recalls. 'But then he also taught me, without me knowing it, quite a few things about the psychology of goalkeeping. By that, I mean the change that occurs when they step on to the field of play. Now, I'm a fairly placid chap off the field. But on the field, if anyone came into contact with me on purpose, then I'd react. Part of that stemmed from Ray but also from my father, who taught me about protection – "knees up, elbows out and, if necessary, bring your head into contact with your opponent at the last minute". I know that seems a bit violent but those were different times.'

What Eric would have given for Dave's dad's advice before he encountered Jack 'The Gunner' Rowley.

Away from football, home was a council house in the Westborough area of Guildford with no central heating and frost on the windows seemingly from November through to March. The four Hollins boys all shared the same bedroom, with John, the youngest, acting as Dave's very own electric blanket.

'Every evening at half-past six I'd say, "John, up you go," and he'd trot upstairs and get into bed,' says Dave. 'Then later on, once he'd got the bed all nice and warm, I'd follow him up and push him over into the cold spot. He's never, ever forgotten that!'

As for school? 'Well, I was never very academic, put it that way. School for me was always more about sport. In fact, our school was very, very competitive when it came to sport. We had one particular sports teacher, Mr Whitney, who was extremely strict but also very good at his job. He was a Welshman who'd been a physical training instructor in the RAF. Years later, after I'd finished my football career, I was walking up the High Street in Guildford and who should be coming the other way but Mr Whitney. It was like meeting a long-lost brother. He was so proud of what I'd gone on and done, especially having played for Wales. Back in the day, he'd been "Sir" – proper respect. Now we were meeting as equals. And it was wonderful.'

Just because Bill Hollins had been a professional goalkeeper didn't, of course, mean that his son was destined to be any good at stopping footballs. It just so happened that he was. Bill's reputation within the game, Dave admits, may well have helped usher him towards Merrow's first team at the tender age of 15. But, once there, it was all about standing on his own two feet.

Before long, Dave noticed a significant improvement in his game. Shots that might once have flown past him were now being saved. Catching crosses under pressure and staying out of the back of the net, rather than being knocked flying into it, became the norm. Instead of seeing him as a soft target, overly physical centre-forwards learned to regard him with a degree of caution, wary of being caught by a tactical knee, elbow or even head-butt. The asthma that ran in the family had cursed him too but could be kept in check with the aid of an inhaler. Suddenly the dream of following in his father's footsteps and playing in goal for a living didn't seem so fanciful after all.

'It's the same dream that so many youngsters have today ... to become a footballer,' Dave confesses. 'That bit never changes. I was at Merrow for around 18 months and towards the end of that time I did start to think perhaps I had something. In those days all goalkeepers were very acrobatic – and I had that too. In many other countries, especially in South America, goalkeepers were often the number-one person that the fans loved to see because they were so acrobatic. It added to the entertainment. Anyway, a few months after I'd gone to Merrow the Brighton manager, Billy Lane, had come down and snatched my elder brother, Roy, to go and play for them. Then, about a year later, he came back … for me!'

Unbeknown to Dave, Brighton & Hove Albion weren't the only ones keeping a close eye on his progress. Portsmouth and Southampton were also interested, together with Guildford City who, by that stage, had lost Ray Drinkwater to the professional game.

For Dave, the choice over where to go was a simple one. Brother Roy was already ensconced in lodgings in Brighton, meaning not only a place to stay but a familiar face to ward off any hint of homesickness. First, Dave had to pass an audition in the shape of a practice match organised by Brighton & Hove Albion for Monday, 1 November 1955, something he now remembers absolutely zilch about. He must have performed well enough as Billy Lane offered him professional terms later that very same week.

Just as when Eric had been handed his first contract by Charlton Athletic, so Dave was under no illusions about where he stood in the goalkeeping pecking order as a 17-year-old at Brighton.

'At that stage it was all about being recognised as someone with talent and being prepared to progress,' he declares. 'More than anything it was the honour, really, of actually playing for a professional club in the Football League. Money didn't come into it at all. I wanted to learn, I wanted to progress and I wanted one day to play first-team football in front of big crowds. I didn't even stop to think about who Brighton's first-choice goalkeeper was. Which, given the incredible run that Eric was on at that time, was probably just as well!'

* * *

There are those of a certain age – usually men, it has to be said – who maintain that success is far easier to come by now in football than it used to be. And to be fair, they may just have a point. Once upon a time, for example, only the winners of domestic leagues went forward to represent their respective countries in the European Cup, football's forerunner to the Champions League, rather than the multiple qualifiers of today. Instead of extra time or penalties after one or maybe two matches, the FA Cup often featured umpteen energy-sapping replays on neutral grounds the length and breadth of the country to decide who progressed from each round.

However, in terms of sheer mountains to climb, you had to go some to beat the ridiculously unfair charade that was the annual scramble for promotion from the lower echelons of the English Football League.

Today, elite football in England and indeed Wales spans four leagues – the Premier League, the Championship, League One and League Two. Up until 1992, they were known simply as the First, Second, Third and Fourth Divisions. Prior to 1958, mind, things were slightly more parochial with the bottom two divisions split along geographical lines. You had Third Division South for 24 clubs situated in the bottom half of the country, and Third Division North for 24 more located above an invisible line stretching roughly from The Wash to a point somewhere between Shrewsbury and Wrexham.

One club per season was promoted from each of the Third Division South and North into the Second Division. One. Solitary. Measly. Pathetic. Club. Finish first, congratulations! Here's your trophy and medals. Finish second, better luck next time.

The stories of injustice under this hopelessly weighted system were many. In 1952, Grimsby Town finished the Third Division North season on 66 points under the two points for a win system, the equivalent of a whopping 95 points today. Alas, they still came second in the table behind Lincoln City. Slaughtered, gutted and heartbroken by the whole experience, Grimsby nevertheless set out to go one better the following campaign but could only finish fifth, a fate that often befell clubs unable to shake off the hangover of missing out on promotion in time to hit the ground running at full pelt the season after.

To the south, a whole raft of what would come to be regarded as pretty successful medium-sized clubs – Southampton, Norwich City, Ipswich Town, Crystal Palace, Queens Park Rangers and Coventry City to name just a few – found their hopes and dreams of mixing with a higher class of clientele reduced to little more than a 4 per cent chance of winning promotion every season.

In 1958, the powers that be finally saw sense and bowed to widespread calls for reform, doing away with the geographical boundary and increasing the number of clubs promoted from the reformed Third Division and the newly created Fourth Division to two per league (a figure that would, in turn, subsequently increase over the years).

Better late than never, Billy Lane could have been forgiven for thinking.

Born William Harry Charles Lohn, in Tottenham, London, on 23 November 1903, Lane had as a young man chosen to change his surname at a time when anti-German sentiment was running high within British society. As a football player he'd been a crack centre-forward, scoring 84 goals in 113 matches for Brentford before transferring to Watford, where he netted 70 times in 125 outings, including a remarkable two-and-a-half-minute hat-trick against Clapton Orient.

Following the Second World War, Lane had, by coincidence, managed Guildford City before being lured to Brighton & Hove Albion in April 1950 as assistant to Don Welsh, the club's then manager. When Welsh defected north to take over as Liverpool's boss in March the following year, the 47-year-old Lane was invited to step into his shoes, initially on a caretaker basis.

As a club, Brighton had serially underperformed up until that point in their history, having never played at a level higher than the Third Division South, but Lane could see there was potential. They were, after all, the only professional Football League outfit at that time in the entire county of Sussex, regularly attracting crowds in excess of 20,000 despite the lack of success on the pitch. Give the people something to actually shout about and that figure, so Lane believed, could rise by 50 per cent, if not more. Which was easier said than done, of course, bearing in mind the borderline mission impossible task of securing promotion from Third Division South, reform being seven long years away.

Nevertheless, having been promoted from caretaker to permanent manager in August 1951, an undaunted Lane duly set his sights on becoming the first man ever to guide Brighton & Hove Albion into the second tier of English football. Almost overnight, true to his innate attacking instincts, Lane did away with the more defensive tactics of his predecessor, adopting an attractive style of play that resulted in goals, improved attendances and a fifth-place finish come the end of the 1951/52 season. Hardly spectacular but a significant improvement on the mid-table obscurity of 12 months previously.

Despite his commitment to attacking football, Lane was far from naïve when it came to the bigger picture. Like so many other managers over the decades, or at least the more successful ones, he recognised that teams needed a framework built along the tried-and-tested goalkeeper/centre-half/midfield/centre-forward backbone. The last man was as important as the front man, in other words.

For longer than anyone could remember, Brighton's goalkeeping position had been the preserve of Harry Baldwin and Jack Ball, two friendly rivals who over the course of 13 war-interrupted years played the lion's share of 400 matches combined. With their best days now behind them, Lane had already started scouring the country for potential replacements when word reached him during the early summer of 1952 that Charlton were releasing Eric Gill, the young stopper he'd seen playing in the quarter-final of the Army Cup two years previously.

Within a matter of hours, having sourced an address for Gill, Lane had sent his 'Catch the 10am train to

Brighton and I'll meet you at the station' telegram. By 11.30 the next morning the two men were sitting opposite each other in one of Lane's favourite restaurants just off the seafront in Preston Street. By mid-afternoon, Eric Gill was a Brighton & Hove Albion player on £13 a week (worth roughly £400 in 2022) during the season (£3 more than he'd been on during his final months at Charlton), dropping to £11 during the off-season.

* * *

Right at the beginning of the Boulting brothers' 1947 film adaptation of Graham Greene's classic 1938 novel *Brighton Rock*, there's a disclaimer. The Brighton that existed between the wars, the one behind the beaches and Regency terraces of 'dark alleyways and festering slums' from where 'the poison of crime and violence and gang warfare began to spread', is a Brighton 'now happily no more'. At least so the viewer is assured.

In reality, the Brighton of the early 1950s, when Eric first set foot in the place, really wasn't that different from the Brighton of the late 1930s. True, the racecourse gangs that had inspired Greene's book were, as the writer himself acknowledged in his second autobiography *Ways of Escape*, 'to all intents quashed for ever as a serious menace at Lewes Assizes a little before the date of my novel'. Yet still the town continued to wear two faces, as indeed it does to this very day: the carefree smile of the day-tripper bound to the frown of the petty (and not-so-petty) criminal. As the novelist and columnist Keith Waterhouse, himself a long-time resident of the Grade II listed Embassy Court on the seafront, once wrote, 'Brighton is a town that always looks as if it is helping police with their inquiries.' And he wasn't wrong.

'I didn't know anything about that so-called seedier side when I first went down there,' insists Eric. 'As I've said, I'd never been to Brighton before in my life. The day that I signed I saw the railway station, a nice posh restaurant, and the football ground where I'd end up spending the happiest years of my playing career. That was enough for me. Once I'd moved there proper, of course I saw more: the seafront; The Lanes with all the little shops; the piers; the beautiful rolling Downs to the north of the town. Forget about gangsters – coming from where I come from, it was like paradise.'

Then again, Eric wasn't exactly some wet-behind-the-ears farm kid. We're talking about a strapping six-foot-tall professional athlete here, raised on the gritty streets of north-west London. Small wonder the shadier side of Brighton life didn't bother him.

And, anyway, he was in love. Ida Dobby had grown up in the block of flats directly opposite Swinley House, London NW1. As kids, her front door faced Eric's front door. He watched her grow up. She watched him grow up. Both liked what they saw. Wedding vows were exchanged on 2 June 1951. Now they had to find somewhere to live in or around Brighton. That somewhere turned out to be a top-floor flat within a house rented by Brighton & Hove Albion on Palmeira Avenue, Hove. Basic would be the word to describe it but, as a stopgap until something better came along, it served its purpose.

'We had the flat at the very top of the house, which was good as we didn't have people going past our door all the time,' says Eric. 'On the floor below us you had Jimmy Leadbetter, an inside-forward who came from Scotland. Below him was Paddy McIlvenny, a lovely, lovely chap who played right-half. Then in the basement you had another Scot, Jimmy Sirrell, an inside-forward who went on to have a pretty good career as a manager. It wasn't the best, to be honest, but it was a start. And Ida was very good about it. Was it what she'd had in mind when we got married? Probably not! But, like so many people after the war, we just took it all in our stride. You tried to make the best of everything. That's what you'd had to do during the war – get on with your lives and hope the bombs didn't hit you. And we were young. You put up with all sorts when you're young.'

Accommodation sorted, Eric turned his attention to the club itself. Today, Brighton & Hove Albion's home is an all mod cons, aesthetically pleasing stadium with the capacity for 30,000-plus spectators. In 1952, things were a tad more primitive. For Palmeira Avenue and all its limitations, see also the Goldstone Ground.

'It wasn't very much, to be honest,' admits Eric with a chuckle. 'Later on they built a proper grandstand the length of the touchline, but back then there was just this tiny little stand somewhere round the halfway line. What you did have were wide-open terraces where everyone used to stand. That's the funny thing – they used to cram more people into the Goldstone than they can get into the new stadium today! Some of the attendances there were huge. Brighton were always fairly high up the league table, so that used to bring the people in. And they'd come in all weathers. It wasn't like today where you have season ticket holders who pay in advance to go. Back then they'd pay on the day at the turnstiles, even if it was raining cats and dogs. It wasn't very much but I loved the place.'

Then there were the training methods, or rather the lack of them.

'It was very, very basic,' Eric declares. 'Everybody – the full-backs, the centre-forwards, goalkeepers, whatever – would do their training together either at the Goldstone or over the local park. Much of that was to do with stamina training, so we'd run laps of the pitch before moving on to sprints. Then the goalkeepers would go to one end of the field and somebody would cross balls at us, that kind of thing. There was no specialist training at all, not like today. Billy Lane had been a centre-forward so goalkeeping wasn't really his thing. It was all left to the trainer, as they were known. That was the same at every club. Our trainer was Joe Wilson, who'd played for Brighton for years before becoming part of the backroom staff. He was a lovely man, Joe, but he wasn't qualified in anything. He wasn't a coach in the way that we know them today, so we used to stick to the basics. But we all liked him. He did his best for us, so we used to try and do our best for him.'

Then there was the state of the Goldstone pitch itself.

'The grounds were in a terrible state,' adds Eric. 'Actually, ours wasn't the worst, but it wasn't the best either. The goalmouths and the centre-circles were always in the poorest states. It was almost accepted that the goalmouths would be muddy and the centre-circles would be muddy, which made it incredibly difficult for goalkeepers. You were playing on it and you were training on it, so the surface never had a chance to recover. Clubs just hadn't yet come to the conclusion that they should have better pitches. Seems strange now, doesn't it?'

Eric made his first-team debut for Brighton on the Goldstone's less than perfect playing surface on Wednesday, 24 September 1952, fellow Palmeira Avenue resident Paddy McIlvenny scoring twice in a 4-2 win over Exeter City that put Albion top of the Third Division South table. Unfortunately, two mistakes on Eric's part contributed towards both Exeter goals. 'Although he didn't have a good match, I am still confident of his abilities to prove to us he is a good goalkeeper,' declared Billy Lane, who, nevertheless, chose to alternate between two other goalkeepers over the four months that followed in the shape of veteran Jack Ball and new signing Harry Medhurst.

'Jackie Ball was a lovely guy, he really was,' says Eric. 'He was nice to me, and he didn't have to be. When someone new comes in, and they're vying for your place in the team, it can get to the point where you don't get on. It's your living and you don't want somebody else to take it away from you. But Jackie wasn't like that. As for Harry, he'd had a good career with Chelsea but he was coming towards the end of his time, as was Jackie. Harry played for a little while but there was one game in particular [a 4-1 defeat to Ipswich Town] where he really wasn't at it. That very same week I'd played for the reserves against Chelsea and saved two penalties. The following Saturday, I was in the first team. It went wrong for Harry and right for me.'

Little did Eric know but he wouldn't miss a single Brighton & Hove Albion first-team match for another five years.

* * *

There's a school of thought that's been allowed to build up over time that suggests the art of goalkeeping in 1950s Britain was pretty ropey. Followers of this school will have you believe it wasn't until the arrival of England's Gordon Banks on the scene the following decade that goalkeepers across the UK began to up the ante. While it's true Banks became the first keeper, certainly in Britain, to thoroughly analyse the position, working overtime after regular training sessions on areas of his game that he felt needed improving, it's also worth remembering that Gordon and his goalkeeping peers of latter years had it considerably easier than Eric and his cohort. In the 1950s the footballs were heavier. The goalmouths were muddier. The challenges from centre-forwards were heftier. You try fielding cannonballs with your bare hands or string gloves while standing ankle-deep in muck waiting to be assaulted. It was, as Eric attests, 'bloody hard, let me tell you'.

Anyway, it's not as if those playing outfield in the 1950s were exactly covering themselves with glory.

'Looking at the cut of the teams as they now enter the bowl that is Wembley, it is almost as if the football of the past is about to meet the football of the future.' So declared the celebrated BBC radio commentator Raymond Glendenning on 25 November 1953 as he observed England's national football team in their heavy cotton shirts and long baggy shorts prepare to take on a Hungarian XI sporting pioneering V-neck collars and low-cut boots.

And, in many ways, he was right. Hungary's 6-3 victory that day in a blur of visionary tactics and one-touch passing blew away the long-held, desperately complacent assertion among the English that they ruled football's waves. Cue an intense period of soul-searching right across the UK regarding the way the game was being played and coached at both club and international levels. Over time, tactics did change. Training grew more varied. Treatment rooms began to actually resemble treatment rooms. Kits became more Hungarian-esque. Footballs got to be lighter, complementing new types of low-cut boots. The steady march towards England's victory in the 1966 World Cup Final had begun. It's just that some of those changes took a little while longer to filter through to football's lower echelons.

'Kick it up to the forwards and they'll score – that was the English and indeed the British way of doing it, but it didn't work like that when the Continentals started getting their act together,' recalls Eric. 'The Hungarians had a lovely style of football that was very fluid, and this wonderful player called Nándor Hidegkuti who sort of floated between midfield and up front. He scored a hat-trick in that game. From then on, we had to take a leaf out of the foreign books in terms of the way we did things. And we did ... sort of. But did I see any improvement in the way we trained at Brighton? Did I see any improvement in the condition of the pitches we played on? I can't say that I did. At least Billy Lane had us playing football rather than just lumping it up the field, so that was something in our favour.'

Admirable as Lane's tactics might have been, in the agricultural world of third-tier football, with so little margin for error in a promotion race where only one club could succeed every year, there was no way of guaranteeing that his way was the right way.

Brighton ended the 1952/53 season in seventh position despite a strong finish that yielded five wins and a draw from their last six matches, a run that helped catapult Eric from the club's third-choice goalkeeper to their undisputed number one. 'Wherever we went and whether we won, lost or drew, we were praised for our standard of play and for our obvious intention of playing football in the highest sense, rather than falling back on hurly-burly tactics in which playing the ball is of a somewhat secondary importance,' said Lane with one eye on what had just gone and the other on the campaign to come. 'We are all out to improve on anything produced last season and I am confident the lads can do it.'

The lads did indeed improve on seventh position the following season, yet it still wasn't enough. Seemingly home and dry in mid-April of 1954 with six matches to go, Brighton somehow managed to stumble as the finishing line came into sight, slipping from first to second (behind eventual champions Ipswich Town) courtesy of two defeats within the space of three days to relegation-threatened Shrewsbury Town and underwhelming draws against Norwich City and Crystal Palace.

To make matters worse, Brighton then allowed the disappointment of missing out on promotion to cloud their form during the early stages of the 1954/55 campaign, nine of their opening 16 league fixtures ending in defeat. The leaves were barely off the trees and already Billy Lane's men were doomed to another season in Third Division South.

'Cor, it was terrible,' remembers Eric. 'To think you played good football all season long only to come second and get nothing. Most teams spent their lives in that division because only one went up. They never knew anything different. And there were some big clubs down there, which made it even harder for the smaller ones to achieve anything. Ipswich always seemed to be around the top places with us and look what they went on to achieve [Ipswich won the First Division title in 1961/62, going on to capture further domestic and European honours in the 1970s and 1980s]. Missing out, especially when you came second, was always a hell of a blow. And, of course, if you didn't get your act together pretty damn quick the season after, then you'd miss out again. Brutal, just brutal.'

If there was a silver lining to this annual procession of despondency, then it came in the ever-improving form of Brighton's last line of defence and Eric's lengthening roll call of world-class saves. The four quite brilliant stops away to Northampton Town in January 1954, which prevented the home team from handing Brighton a thrashing on a rare off day for Lane's team. The acrobatic leap to deny Aldershot inside-forward Billy Durkin at the Goldstone Ground in April 1954, once described to me by the late, lifelong Brighton supporter Arthur Nightingale as the finest save he'd seen in 50 years of watching football. Clawing a John Atyeo header from point-blank range over the crossbar at the Goldstone in October 1954, a feat met with a clap of admiration from the prolific Bristol City and England striker. The outstanding close-range reaction save at Watford in April 1955, which had opposition centre-forward Maurice Cook shaking his head in disbelief at what he'd just witnessed. The trio of outstanding saves the very same month away to Aldershot, which earned Brighton's goalkeeper a standing ovation from the home fans as he left the field.

Such was Eric's form throughout 1955 that many observers of the game in England began talking about him as one of the very best goalkeepers in the country. Lane himself went as far as saying that, in his considered opinion based on recent form, only Gil Merrick of Birmingham City and Manchester City's Bert Trautmann were better bets between the posts. All of which begs a question: why didn't one of England's or indeed Wales's leading clubs of the time come in for him?

The simple answer is that several did – top-flight Portsmouth and Cardiff City among them. It's just that Eric was never told about it.

'If another club was interested in you, then you'd be the last to know,' says Eric. 'That's the way it was then. You had no agents or anyone working away on your behalf. It was just you and you alone. The only time you were ever told anything is if your club wanted to get rid of you. Then they'd say something like: "Oh, so and so is interested in you. Why don't you go and talk to them?" When you heard that, you knew your time was up. I did hear murmurs that I was being looked at but that's all they were – murmurs. I wouldn't have gone anyway. I'd made up my mind by then that I was going to stay and settle in Brighton.'

There was a good reason for that, besides football.

'I had a very good friend who once said to me, "What are you going to do when you pack it in, Eric?" And I said, "I've got no idea. I've never thought about it. I want to go

66

on playing for as long as I can." He said, "Well, I think you should start thinking about it. God forbid you should have to pack up soon, but it'd be good to have something in reserve." This guy's name was Colin Lux. His daughter, Carol, used to stand behind the goal in what was called the North Stand and I was her favourite player. We went round to theirs one night for supper and that's when he said, "Why don't you get yourself a guest house?" He had a small hotel himself. He goes, "It's a good idea, a guest house. You've got everything paid for. You've got your accommodation, your food, the lot." That's where the idea of setting up my own business came from.'

It just so happened that an 11-bedroom guest house called The Perrimay had come on the market in Charlotte Street to the east of Brighton town centre. Eric and Ida went to have a look and liked what they saw, but there was a problem – even with his wages, they didn't have enough in the bank to afford it. At which point, as Eric recalls with a smile, their fairy godmother stepped in.

'We said to the woman who owned it, "It's lovely, but we just haven't got the money." And she said, "Well how much have you got?" And it went from there. She ended up lending me quite a lot of money to buy it. She said to us, "I'm doing it because your wife should have this business." She just seemed to gel with Ida. She said, "I'd like her to have it." So, we used our savings plus what money we could get on the mortgage, and the rest she lent to us. She was ever so good to us, she really was. A lovely lady.'

And so Eric and Ida moved out of Palmeira Avenue and into Charlotte Street, Ida taking on most of the day-to-day running of The Perrimay from the get-go. With

Eric's goalkeeping career approaching its zenith and his wages covering both the mortgage and the previous owner's benevolence, there was simply no other way. All the money he earned went back into the business. It was hard work but they were happy.

Brighton & Hove Albion, however, weren't.

'It was my first business and I was quite excited, but the club, and in particular Billy Lane, really didn't like it,' says Eric. 'I was the first player they'd ever had who'd bought his own business and the thought of that unsettled them. Billy Lane even came down and took a look around the place, although he didn't tell me. I only found out later. Don't forget in those days we were virtually prisoners to our clubs. They could do anything they liked with us. If a player became independent in any way, then that meant they had less control over them. I think Billy Lane thought I'd become more independent of the club and wouldn't have to bow down to him as much as we were supposed to. Once I'd shown that running The Perrimay didn't affect my performances on the football field, then it wasn't so much of an issue. But it was always there, in the background.'

A footballer, certainly in the UK, is rarely busier than they are during what you might call traditional holiday times. Today, the festive, new year and Easter periods continue to be stuffed full of matches. In the 1950s, things were even more congested. That's because along with Boxing Day, New Year's Day, Good Friday and Easter Monday, football was also played on Christmas Day.

To make matters even more convoluted, the concept of keeping fixtures relatively local during the holidays didn't exist. For instance, Eric's first Christmas Day match for Brighton & Hove Albion came the better part of 200 miles away at Walsall in 1953, with the return fixture between the two clubs being played, as was customary, just 24 hours later on Boxing Day. In other words when The Perrimay was at its busiest, Eric often wasn't there, increasing the workload on Ida.

'It seems odd now, playing on Christmas Day, but we just accepted it,' reflects Eric. 'I think we were all just happy to be playing football and to be in a team, the first team at that, because if you weren't in the first team then you'd be paid less money. As long as you were in the first team, everything was fine. At Christmas you had to forego your traditional puddings and nice things like that. Football came first. It had to because you wanted to keep your place in the team and that meant keeping fit. It also meant not seeing your family because there was so much travelling involved. If you were playing a long way away on Christmas Day, then that meant being gone on Christmas Eve too. At The Perrimay, we had staff, but my wife took the burden of it. There were loads of times I left her in it while I went off to play football. But she was good with that. She was marvellous. She made it the success it became.'

On Saturday, 26 February 1955, Eric ran out at the Goldstone Ground to face Colchester United in what would be his 100th consecutive match for Brighton. The milestone made little news outside the county of Sussex but was treated with the respect it deserved closer to home, Eric being handed the club captaincy for the day in recognition of his achievement. In 1955 there was no such thing as squad rotation. If you were fit, then you played. Seen through a 21st-century lens, 100 back-to-back appearances might not appear that significant. Except, as we've already touched on in these pages, football was a far more physical animal then. A player might be fortunate to make 30 or 40 appearances in a row without missing the occasional match due to injury, let alone 100. With that in mind, Eric's century starts to be seen in a different light.

'I got the captaincy on a couple of occasions and, yeah, it was very nice,' he admits with unabashed pride. 'It's a bit special for a goalkeeper to lead the team out and then go up the middle to toss the coin with the referee. Goalkeepers never used to be made captains. They still aren't – well, very, very rarely. They say we like to keep our heads down and just get on with the job in hand. And we do. But who doesn't enjoy a little bit of fame? You know, seeing your name in the papers and that. I know I did!'

As a goalkeeper, Eric was at the top of his game. He'd bought a business. He had an adoring wife who knew as much, if not more, about running that business than he ever would. Post-war rationing was finally over. A summer heatwave lay just around the corner, meaning full rooms for weeks on end at The Perrimay.

Life couldn't, it's fair to say, have been better for Eric Gill.

4

MR CONSISTENT

*'We are what we repeatedly do. Excellence, then,
is not an act, but a habit.'* – Aristotle

THERE ARE some people – you know, those authority-on-everything types who speak almost entirely in soundbites – who would have you believe that 'you never get a second chance to make a first impression'.

They are, you may not be so surprised to learn, talking flim-flam. And Eric Gill and Dave Hollins are living proof of that.

Eric might have been at the top of his game in 1955 but that didn't prevent Billy Lane, like all good football managers, from having one eye on the future. Through his contacts in the Guildford area, Lane had learned about a nippy right-winger called Roy Hollins doing exciting things on the flanks at Merrow. Long story short, he signed Roy. In time, Lane discovered Roy had a younger brother who played in goal. He had the brother watched, received positive feedback and arranged for him to feature in a practice match during the first week of November 1955 (the one mentioned in the previous chapter that Dave now has absolutely no recollection of). Within days, 17-year-old Dave Hollins was in possession of his first professional football contract worth £7.50 per week (equivalent to about £210 in 2022) during the playing season.

Can Dave remember meeting Eric Gill for the first time on arriving at the Goldstone Ground? Absolutely not.

Can Eric recall coming face to face with Dave on the young pretender's inaugural day at the club? That would be a no.

There may have been handshakes. There may have been introductions. There may even have been conversations. Or there might not. Either way, contrary to what those authority-on-everything types might say, no trumpets sounded. Mind you, it wasn't long before they did start to get to know each other.

'Once I'd seen him play, I thought, *This guy is not a bad goalkeeper*, even at that relatively young age,' recalls Eric. 'We'd had others there that were ordinary, but with Dave it was a case of, *No, this one is a bit different. He's going to be a good goalie.* Like all good goalkeepers he always seemed to get himself in the right positions at the right time. That's an art you can't teach people. And he was a nice guy – he still is a nice guy – and that made it hard for me not to get on with him. So, we became friends.'

'You've got to remember that I was only an apprentice,' adds Dave. 'We cleaned the boots of the first-team players, swept the terracing, assisted the groundsman and things like that. We were pretty low on the ground. In fact, it was like we were segregated from the senior players. There was this hierarchy. But I liked to make sure I knew people.

It's part of my personality, always has been, and because of that I do sort of remember talking to Eric fairly early on. It might have been when I was sweeping the terracing and the first team were lapping the track that went around the pitch. They were a friendly lot, the senior players, lads like winger Frankie Howard, who was the joker in the pack, and right-back Des Tennant, who took the meanest free kicks. You really didn't want to be in goal when he lined one up against you.

'Then you had Eric, this phenomenal goalkeeper in the middle of this incredible run of unbroken games. On the field, he was always very assured. His timing was perfect. When he came out to catch a cross, he would always catch that cross. We actually had different styles. I was probably more agile, a Peter Bonetti [the late Chelsea and England keeper] type of goalkeeper, only I wasn't as good as Peter. Today, it seems all goalkeepers have to play the same way, more like sweepers than goalkeepers. The positions they take up are completely alien to me. Back then, you had room for different kinds of goalkeepers like Eric and me. Clubs weren't going to get rid of you because you didn't use both feet or couldn't control a ball like Bobby Moore. Off the field, I soon came to realise that Eric was a very honest, straight man with this almost gentlemanly air about him, always absolutely immaculate in his appearance. And that hasn't changed about him.'

'Oh yes, I am like that, even now,' Eric concurs. 'Well, there's no point being scruffy, is there? It's a suit, collar and tie for special occasions and smart casual otherwise. I never went for hats, maybe a cap when it's cold and windy. Dapper – that's what I tried to be. I got it from my mum and dad who always tried to look their best no matter what the circumstances. Appearances count, or at least they should.'

Promising though he undoubtedly was, Dave's first couple of years at Brighton & Hove Albion would mirror Eric's experiences at Charlton Athletic during the late 1940s. We're talking 'A' team football for the thirds in backwaters such as Gravesend, Newbury and Windsor, along with, once he'd turned 18 in February 1956, tiptoeing through the potential minefield that was peacetime conscription.

By now Roy Hollins had already seen his career as a professional footballer go up in smoke due to a succession of knee injuries suffered during National Service. If Dave was going to emerge unscathed, then he would be needing the same sort of guardian angel with a military rank who had stepped in to help Eric.

That angel duly materialised once Dave had completed his basic training and been assigned to the Royal Army Medical Corps based at Netley Hospital, a vast military establishment near Southampton. Once a month, a box of cigars and a stash of match tickets would arrive at Netley addressed to Dave's commanding officer courtesy of Billy Lane. In exchange, Dave was released to play for Brighton & Hove Albion and generally kept away from what you might call danger.

This ruse worked just fine until, with two weeks of his service left to go, Dave's guardian angel was transferred and replaced by a different commanding officer.

'I was walking out of the gate with my little holdall,' Dave recalls, 'off to play at Leicester in the Combination

League, I think, and all of a sudden, this voice said, "Oi! Where are you going?" I said, "Well, I'm going home." He said, "Can you submit your pass?" And I couldn't because it had been arranged out of sight by the CO who, unbeknown to me, had since been transferred. What I was trying to do was actually illegal. So, I ended up being confined to barracks for 11 days.'

Those last two weeks excepted, Dave describes his time in service as 'a great experience', and not only because he continued to play football for Brighton. It taught him the value of hard work. It taught him about comradeship, 26 lads in their late teens sharing a barrack room, all equally committed to helping one another get through the dreaded Monday morning inspections. More importantly, it taught him something about first aid, the value of which would only truly come to pass years later on two separate occasions.

'I was on holiday in Italy with the family when this bloke went into the swimming pool, in the deep end, in freezing cold water and went under,' says Dave. 'I suddenly realised he was drowning. So, I dived in, hauled him out, got him on to the concrete on the side and started pumping water out of him. Saved his life, in other words. Then – I can't remember how much later – I was back in England, in Guildford, on the banks of the River Wey, and I heard this chap shouting, "Help!" Everyone was just looking around, stargazing. So, I jumped in, got this old boy out and started pumping him. A young lad had seen what was going on from the other side of the river and jumped in as well to help, except that when he got to where we were he trod on a glass bottle. So, there I am with the old boy, while at the same time trying to stop the blood pumping out of this young lad's foot using my shirt, which I'd taken off. And all the while people are just looking on, not bothering to do anything in the slightest. I couldn't have done any of that without the basic life-saving skills that I learned in my Royal Army Medical Corps training.'

* * *

Dave's arrival at the Goldstone Ground during the 1955/56 season coincided with Brighton's most determined tilt yet at winning promotion from the Third Division South. Their form throughout the entire campaign, especially at home, was little short of astonishing (20 wins from 23 league matches at the Goldstone Ground). Many of those victories were about as emphatic as they come: 5-2 against Aldershot, 5-0 against Southampton, 4-0 against Southend United, 6-0 against Norwich City, 4-0 against Northampton Town, 5-0 against Crystal Palace, 5-0 against Gillingham, 4-1 against Bournemouth, 4-1 against Newport County (hot on the heels of an 8-1 win over the Welsh club in the first round of the FA Cup).

It's not as if they were slouches away from home either. 'The Brighton team, certainly a great side, looked like the pick of Russia, Hungary and Uruguay put together,' gushed the reporter from the *Exeter Express & Echo* after Billy Lane's team had demolished Exeter City 5-0 in the west country during November.

Ultimately, the race for the coveted first place boiled down to three frontrunners: Brighton, Leyton Orient and Ipswich Town (relegated the previous season from the Second Division, having only clinched promotion from the Third Division South in 1954). On 31 March, Brighton won 1-0 at Leyton Orient, the return match between the two clubs three weeks later finishing 1-1 in front of a crowd officially given as 30,864 yet widely reckoned to be close on 40,000. The first of those fixtures had seen Eric produce a save that, during my own early days supporting Brighton in the late 1970s, I heard older fans describe as the greatest ever produced by an Albion goalkeeper.

Phil Woosnam's first-time strike with three minutes of normal time to go is on its way into the far corner of Brighton's net.

Eric Gill is unsighted. By the time he sees the ball coming through a crowd of players it's four or maybe five feet from crossing the line.

Undaunted, Eric's innate reflexes send him arcing through the air to his right. Out comes a hand, a 'strong hand' in goalkeeping lingo. He deflects the ball around the post. Orient, to the amazement of just about everyone in the ground, have a corner kick, not a goal.

Seven days after the second Leyton Orient match, Brighton travelled to Ipswich to play their penultimate league fixture of the season. They lost 2-1. Ultimately, the result only benefited Leyton Orient, enabling the London club to edge both Brighton and Ipswich to first place in the final reckoning (by one and two points, respectively).

Brighton had 29 wins, 73 goals scored at home, 39 goals scored away, 65 points in total (the equivalent of 94 under today's three points for a win system), all for what?

'You tell me,' says Eric with a shrug of his shoulders, the memory of yet another second-place finish as painful now as it was back in 1956. 'That's when you start getting to the point where you think, *Are we ever going to do this? Is it ever going to happen?* Because you can only go on trying for so long before you miss the boat altogether. We had good players in that team who deserved to be playing in a higher division, but they weren't getting the opportunity. That was a real shame. All we could do was keep on trying.'

When Brighton then lost six of their opening 15 league fixtures the following season, pretty much torpedoing any hopes of promotion for another year, the fans didn't so much revolt as finally find a voice for their own frustrations.

In an October edition of Brighton's matchday programme, Billy Lane wrote:

> I would like supporters to know that I am responsible for giving you entertainment on the field on match days, so please do not blame the directors, players, trainers or staff if you are disappointed at the team's recent display. For a moment, look back at the majority of matches you have seen at the Goldstone during recent years. Have you been satisfied? I am sure all sportsmen would agree with me that they have enjoyed most of the games, but perhaps a little disappointed at the club not gaining promotion.

The club has been criticised for not doing this or that, not wanting promotion, etc, but as loyal supporters, as I know you are, do be a little patient and not in too much of a hurry in voicing your opinions or condemning the players. Blame me as you care to, but please give encouragement to the lads and you will notice how this will improve their play.

Much later, Lane would admit privately to friends that 1956 was his most disappointing year in a lifetime of football, one in which he felt the pressures of management tipping over into his personal life for the first time. Convinced that nobody else could do a better job, he nevertheless stayed resolutely in post, finding solace in his family and faith (besides attending church every Sunday, Lane was also an occasional lay preacher). Resigning simply never entered his mind.

Being a relative newcomer to the club, the deep disappointment of missing out on promotion yet again was lost on young Dave Hollins, residing in what he still describes as 'dreamland' following his arrival from Merrow. Anyhow, besides learning his trade as a goalkeeper, he had other things to contend with in the shape of the Royal Army Medical Corps. Throughout 1956 and 1957, thanks to the benevolence/negligence/call it what you will of his commanding officer, Dave was able to juggle his career alongside conscription, although the lion's share of his time was spent at Netley.

National Service completed, Dave took one look at his digs in the Brighton suburb of Portslade and decided enough was enough. On arriving from Merrow in November 1955, he'd lodged in a house alongside brother Roy and two South African players, Eric Hodge and Denis Foreman, the latter an immensely talented left-sided player who would clock up 69 goals in 219 appearances for Brighton as well as playing cricket for Sussex as a decent middle-order batsman.

'When I got back from National Service it just wasn't the same and I got a bit fed up with the place,' Dave recalls. 'They had cats everywhere that would climb all over the food. I knew Eric had his guest house in Charlotte Street, so one day I said to him, "Any chance of me staying at your place?" And he said, "Sure, come on over." So I did. I was there probably 18 months, maybe even two years.'

Two rivals for one position living under the one roof for two years. Didn't that seem, er, a bit bizarre?

'Not at all,' says Eric. 'In fact, it made perfect sense. He needed a place to live.'

'I can't say that it did, no,' agrees Dave.

Alright then, but wasn't there a danger that they might have fallen out, or got on each other's nerves?

'Noooooo!' says Eric. 'It was okay. We got on fine. We've always got on just fine. There was never any animosity between us at all, even when we were competing over the same shirt.'

'Charlotte Street was a home away from home for me – that's how important it was,' adds Dave. 'I looked up to Eric almost like an older brother. He was a stabling influence, not that I really needed it, so being around him helped me as I found my way during the early part of my career. Then you had Ida, his wife, who was marvellous.

She'd bring me up a cup of tea every morning and generally make sure I was looking after myself and eating well. It was everything I could have wished for.'

On Saturday, 18 February 1956, Eric had marked his 150th consecutive league and cup match in a Brighton shirt with three outstanding saves in a 2-0 win away to Reading. Seven months later he surpassed the previous Albion record for back-to-back appearances – 175 – held by Billy Hayes, another goalkeeper who'd played for the club in the years immediately after the First World War. Five months after that, on 23 February 1957, Eric made it to 200, captaining the team for the second time in his Brighton career in a 1-0 win over Southampton at the Goldstone Ground.

At which point the national press, as well as the regional hacks, began to sense an unfolding story.

'Two hundred became a real big target of mine,' says Eric. 'That was quite a number and, once I got there, that's when it really started to mean something to me. I think that's when I also became conscious of the record because it started to appear in the papers quite a lot. You know, "Eric Gill, the goalkeeper, playing his two-hundredth consecutive match", "Eric Gill, the goalkeeper, playing his two-hundred-and-tenth consecutive match", "Eric Gill, the goalkeeper, playing his two-hundred-and-twentieth consecutive match". Whenever anyone was covering one of our games, it would get mentioned in the match report. And the nearer I got, the more they wrote about it. For me, it was usually about taking it one game at a time. I never looked any further ahead than that. But, yeah, the closer I got, the more I did start to think about it.'

The record Eric became increasingly conscious of, the one for the longest unbroken run of matches played by a goalkeeper in the Football League, belonged to Ted Ditchburn, last line of defence for Tottenham Hotspur and occasionally England. Between April 1948 and March 1954, Ditchburn had appeared in 247 consecutive league and cup matches for Spurs, a figure that, given football's physical nature, was believed at the time to be unsurpassable.

Could Eric do it? Barring injury or a sudden unexpected loss of form, there seemed to be no reason why not.

As for the secret, or rather secrets, behind Eric's remarkable endurance?

'Consistency,' said Denis Foreman, now sadly deceased, of Eric when I interviewed him in 2005 for a piece about his memories of playing football and cricket during the 1950s and 1960s. 'That might sound obvious, but to be that consistent over such a long period of time takes something. We had a lot of players in different positions who were very consistent – we needed to in order to keep on challenging towards the top of the league. But Eric gave us that foundation. And it all starts from the back in football, as you often hear people say.'

'I didn't make my Brighton debut until 1958 but I'd been going to the Goldstone as a supporter with my father for quite a few years before then,' says Adrian Thorne, who played 84 times for the club as a centre-forward, scoring 44 goals in the process. 'Eric was so dependable that it was easy to overlook his overall contribution to the team. You expected him to perform at a consistently high standard, so when he made a mistake it would come as something of a shock. It helped that the supporters loved him too. You want the supporters to be behind you, to sing your name, and they were always right behind Eric.'

'Brighton were known as a good footballing side and I think that probably helped Eric,' said Thorne's former strike partner John Shepherd, another who's sadly no longer with us, when he and I sat down to talk football in 2014. 'As a goalkeeper, if you're surrounded by good footballers who can play a bit, then that gives you more options in terms of what you do with the ball. It also allows you to get on with your job, safe in the knowledge that everybody else on the field knows theirs. Eric just happened to be very good at his job which, in turn, inspired his team-mates.'

'I think he's right about being surrounded by good players,' concurs Eric of Shepherd's assessment. 'I was, and that did give me more options. I could kick with either foot as well, which also worked in my favour. I always kicked dead balls with my right foot, my stronger one, but when I had it in my hands I could kick with my left and reach the halfway line no problem. That was useful when you had a forward standing in your face, harassing you – which they would do a lot – thinking you could only kick with your right foot, and you'd go left and surprise them.'

Consistent. Dependable. Loved by the fans. A good player surrounded by other good players. It helped as well that Eric, at no point in his entire career, endured one of those spells that every footballer, regardless of their position, absolutely dreads, a period when their form deserts them entirely.

'I wasn't infallible, but I never had a bad run, no,' he says with a justifiable hint of pride in his voice. 'I always believed in myself, that I could do my job. When I did make a mistake, I could get over it. I wasn't one of those players who lets a mistake play on their mind and ends up making more mistakes. You'd know people would be looking at you, thinking, "He shouldn't have done that." I just said to myself, *Right, you made a mistake there. Don't do that again.* Or I'd think, *Why did I do that?* and then go away and work on it. I probably worked hardest on my angles. By that, I mean cutting angles down when players come at you from the wings, making sure they have nothing to aim at. I put an awful lot of thought into that. It's not just a case of standing there and trying to stop the ball when it comes at you. It's about being in the right place to enable you to stop it.'

So what, in Eric's considered opinion, makes a good goalkeeper?

'You've got to anticipate where you think the other player is going to shoot or play the ball. It's as simple as that. If you can sort of think, *I know where this is going to go*, and get yourself into that space as quickly as you can, then you're on your way. Once you're playing regularly, you get to know opposing players and what they do and how they do it. I used to make mental notes to remember what they did. For instance, with penalties, most penalty takers put them in the same place all the time. You need to think, *This one puts it to the left*, and remember how they do it. It's all on videos and laptops now but it was memories in my day. Oh, and you've got to enjoy it. The more you enjoy being a goalkeeper, the better you'll get. If you get too serious about anything in life, it can harm you.'

There was, of course, one supreme irony to Eric's durability. Just as Sam Bartram had stalled Eric's progress at Charlton Athletic, so history was in danger of repeating itself as Dave Hollins struggled to break through at Brighton. There comes a time in every professional goalkeeper's development when he, or she, is ready for first-team football. Dave, 19 years old as of 4 February 1957, had long since reached that point. Did it ever cross his mind that he might never get the opportunity?

If it did, then he's far too positive a person, even now, to admit it.

'At that stage it was still all about progression,' Dave maintains. 'You just keep on learning your trade in the reserves and in training, trying your best to improve. In the back of your mind, you tell yourself, *At some point my chance will come.* That's the way you have to think.'

Which is all very well and good spoken decades later with hindsight. When you're 19, and impatient, and you want the rest of your life to start, except it won't, even though you're beyond ready for lift-off, then you can only imagine the pent-up frustration. Team sports the world over are littered with poor unfortunates who, no matter how much effort they put in, never got to step out of the shadows and make their full debuts. Because of competition for places. Because of injury. Because of a change in manager. Because of budget cuts. Because they grew tired of hanging around and, quite literally, took their eye off the ball. Wait too long and, in the relatively short lifespan of the average professional footballer, the team bus might just leave without you. For good.

'At some point my chance will come.' So Dave reminded himself day after day, week after week, month after month as his friend, rival and landlord kept on keeping on.

But would it, really?

5

THE BEST OF TIMES,
THE WORST OF TIMES

'There is a phrase "the sweet smell of success".
And I can only tell you I've had two experiences
of that and it smells like Brighton and oyster
bars and things like that.' – Laurence Olivier

IT'S SATURDAY, 24 August 1957 in the bottom
right-hand county of England. Brighton & Hove Albion
are away to Gillingham on the opening day of the new
football season in what is Eric Gill's 213th consecutive
match between the posts for the club. Midway through
the second half, Eric collects the ball and bounces it to
the edge of his penalty area. He looks up, spots team-mate
Peter Harburn in space and gives it an almighty punt in his
direction. The ball clears every outfield player on the pitch
as it sails downfield through the Kent air, leaving Harburn
one-on-one with the Gillingham goalkeeper. Harburn,
a big, powerful centre-forward who joined Brighton
straight out of the Royal Navy, loves nothing better than
an eyeball-to-eyeball duel with an opposing keeper (and

has the missing teeth to prove it). The final bounce is a kind one on a springy playing surface that's benefited from a couple of months' summer respite. Harburn rises and heads the ball beyond the onrushing goalie into the back of Gillingham's net for the only goal of the match. Brighton are up and running with a win. Just the 45 league matches remaining to seal that elusive promotion from the Third Division South.

* * *

Eric's colossal punts weren't the only thing in the air in 1957. In October the Soviet Union would fire the starter pistol on the space race by launching Sputnik 1, the first artificial satellite ever to orbit Earth. On the ground young people – 'teenagers' – were ruffling the feathers of their elders. Frank Sinatra, Tony Bennett and Perry Como were out. Elvis Presley, Buddy Holly and Gene Vincent were in. Grey suits and dowdy frocks were history, superseded by long narrow jackets with velvet lapels and colourful skirts puffed out by layers of petticoats. If the 'Teddy boy' look didn't float your boat then you could always become a leather-clad rocker. Skiffle, scooter, sexpot, flick knife and album were among the year's new words and expressions, along with beatnik and angry young man, thanks in part to the publication of Jack Kerouac's *On the Road* and John Braine's *Room at the Top*, respectively. The times really were a-changin', even if Bob Dylan was still seven years away from telling everyone about it.

In Britain, football was also undergoing a transformation of its own. In April it was announced by the Treasury that the sport would, finally, be exempted from paying what was known as entertainment tax, a 'temporary' levy introduced by the government in 1916 to help raise funds to pay for the First World War (and which had bled many clubs in the lower leagues to the point of bankruptcy, forcing them to sell their better players). December would see the last full league programme of matches played on Christmas Day as the arrival of floodlights and evening fixtures reduced the need for matches to be squeezed into public holidays, enabling supporters to stay at home with their families on the Yuletide.

Perhaps the most significant change, certainly as regards the potential fortunes of Brighton & Hove Albion, involved the announcement during the summer that the Football League were to abolish the Third Division South and Third Division North as of the 1958/59 season, replacing them with new national Third and Fourth Divisions. Two clubs per season would go up from the Third to the Second Division, with four ascending from the Fourth to the Third. For the larger, more ambitious English and Welsh clubs marooned in the lower leagues, this long overdue reorganisation came as manna from heaven. At long last, finishing second would mean promotion, albeit not for another season.

Awopbopaloobopalopbamboom, as Little Richard was fond of saying.

Four days after heading his winning goal at Gillingham, Harburn scored again in the 2-1 home win over Bournemouth (or Bournemouth & Boscombe Athletic, as they were known until 1971), consolidating Brighton's decent start to the campaign. 'This evening we greet all supporters, old and new, and trust this season will be THE SEASON for the Albion', wrote Billy Lane in his notes for the match programme. Throughout the remainder of 1957 and the early weeks of 1958, his players largely maintained their good form, ensuring they went to bed most Saturday nights top of the table.

Things didn't always go quite to plan though. At Swindon on Christmas Day, the team emerged from their hotel to discover that the taxis booked to take them to the ground hadn't materialised, leaving no alternative but to make the journey on foot. They arrived on the stroke of kick-off time and, under the circumstances, did well to earn a 2-2 draw. However, in the main, perhaps more than at any other point in the club's history, Brighton were looking good to finish top of the Third Division South.

On the afternoon of Thursday, 6 February, Albion's players had just finished a double training session ahead of their forthcoming home fixture against Southampton when, a little after 3.30pm, news broke that an aircraft carrying the Manchester United team home from a European Cup tie against Red Star Belgrade of Yugoslavia had crashed following a stopover in Munich. Those Brighton players who hadn't already showered, changed and departed immediately gathered around a wireless in one of the Goldstone Ground's back offices. Details were sketchy, but the aircraft appeared to have careered off the end of the runway before exploding. People had died, that much was for certain.

With every subsequent news bulletin that afternoon and evening (and indeed over the following days), so the low-down got worse. The plane had crashed in snowy conditions on its third attempt at take-off, and 23 of the

44 people on board the chartered Elizabethan aircraft, including seven of the players, were dead. Manager Matt Busby was on a life-support machine. Duncan Edwards, sometimes referred to by his Manchester United team-mate Bobby Charlton as 'the greatest', was also in hospital, although doctors rated his chances of survival as good (wrongly, as it would turn out, the midfielder's immense physical strength belying the true extent of his injuries). From the Old Shoreham Road, on which the Goldstone Ground stood, to Old Trafford, the whole of Britain went into collective shock.

'I was walking down Deansgate in my home city of Manchester when I spotted this newspaper billboard,' recalled future Brighton midfielder Nobby Lawton in 2005 of the moment when, as an 18-year-old Manchester United youth team player, his adolescent world temporarily stopped turning. 'On it was written something to do with a plane crash in Munich. I bought a copy. Everybody was buying copies. And we all stood in silence. I just couldn't believe what I was reading. I don't think anybody could. All of those boys ... dead. And others fighting for their lives, including Matt. It was just too much to take in.'

Back in Sussex, Dave Sexton, scorer of Albion's second goal against Swindon Town on Christmas Day, departed the Goldstone Ground convinced Saturday's match against Southampton would be postponed. Sexton had no connections with anyone at Manchester United, other than being part of what's often still referred to as the wider 'football family'. That didn't stop him being, he would recollect, 'overcome with an immense sense of grief, the kind I'd never felt before outside of my own family'.

In the event, the Southampton match did go ahead, with spectators observing a period of silence prior to kick-off. Just short of 20 years later, Sexton, a keen student of the game even as a young man, would become Manchester United's manager, appointing Harry Gregg – one of the survivors from the plane crash – as his goalkeeping coach.

Like Sexton, Eric had no close links to anyone at Manchester United, but that didn't stop him experiencing similar pangs of grief. He had, after all, made his first-class debut as a goalkeeper at Old Trafford back in 1951 and retained a strong sense of affection, like so many others in the game, for Matt Busby and his ability to build young, exciting, attacking football teams.

'It was terrible,' says Eric. 'God, we lost some great players that day. I do remember thinking it was a miracle that any of them managed to get out of it alive. I mean, you don't tend to survive an aeroplane crash, do you? To think that Bobby Charlton, Harry Gregg and some of the others not only lived but carried on playing in the years afterwards is nothing short of remarkable. I'm not a particularly religious person but things like that do make you wonder – an aeroplane full of players, and some get to survive, and some don't. Who decides that then?'

The Munich air disaster cast a huge shadow over the remaining three months of the domestic 1957/58 football calendar. 'It really was as if the whole country went into this deep sense of mourning,' is how Dave Hollins remembers it. Football was far less tribal in the 1950s than it is today. Manchester United had been representing England in the European Cup. Everyone – yes, even Manchester City supporters – wanted them to win it. National pride was at stake at a time when the Second World War was still fresh in people's minds. Consequently, the pain of what happened at Munich, despite being at its most intense in and around Manchester, was felt nationwide.

As insignificant as it may seem in the grand scheme of things, and as corny as it sounds, football does have healing qualities. In the immediate days and weeks after Munich, supporters of all clubs found solace in being together. They held collections for the bereaved families at matches, journeyed many miles across the country to line the streets at the funerals and stood alongside Manchester United fans at matches to show solidarity. Some found light relief reading about Brighton's goalkeeper as he closed in on a small piece of football history, a positive story doing the rounds at a pretty dark time. Sixteen days after the disaster, Brighton beat Walsall 2-0 at home in a match that saw Eric equal Ted Ditchburn's record of 247 consecutive appearances.

At which point all eyes turned towards Highfield Road, home of Coventry City, where on Saturday, 1 March Eric would, all things being well, create a new Football League record for the longest unbroken run of matches ever played by a goalkeeper.

The week leading up to the trip to Coventry was unlike any Eric had experienced before or indeed since. Suddenly he was well and truly in the spotlight, a place many goalkeepers – by nature quite modest, reserved creatures – aren't entirely comfortable with. Nevertheless, Eric went along with it all, politely fielding requests from members of the media keen to document his story, including the long arm of the BBC World Service. Among the congratulatory mail that poured into the Goldstone Ground was a telegram from none other than Ted Ditchburn, saluting Eric's impending achievement. Away from the media circus he trained hard, as usual, alongside his team-mates. Physically, he felt good.

Or at least he did until the Thursday. It was then, from out of nowhere, that the aching and sweating began. Eric trained that day, doing his best to mask the fact that he didn't feel 100 per cent from his team-mates and, above all, Billy Lane. Afterwards he returned immediately to Charlotte Street and his bed, hoping a long sleep would somehow put things right.

It didn't. Come Friday morning, seemingly every bone in Eric's body hurt. Even getting out of bed was an effort. Friday morning was, however, when the team sheet always went up at the Goldstone Ground for any match on a Saturday. Had Lane rumbled him at training the previous day? Should he come clean about feeling, frankly, like shit? Either way, Eric knew he had no alternative but to go in.

On arrival, Lane took one look at his first-choice goalkeeper and told him to go back to bed. The time had finally come for Brighton's second-choice keeper to step out from the shadows.

'I was sick as a post, mentally as well as physically,' admits Eric. 'To think I played all that time and then had to drop out of the team, not because I'd been dropped or was injured, but because I had flu. "No, I can't let you play, you're going back to bed" – that's what Bill Lane said. And, of course, he was right. Whether I was trying to change his mind, or bluff it, I honestly don't know, but he made the right decision. I didn't think so at the time, but he did. We were chasing promotion so he had to be careful. Imagine if I had played and I'd cost us the game – that wouldn't have been right. There was too much riding on it. So, I went home, pulled the sheets over my head and stayed there. It was a big, big disappointment, I can tell you.'

Twenty-four hours later, Eric turned up at Brighton station before the team set off by train for Coventry and tried to convince Lane that he was, in fact, fit to play. Today, he has no memory of this happening (and neither, for that matter, has Dave). One thing Eric can recall, though, is taking time to send a telegram to Ted Ditchburn informing the Tottenham goalkeeper that his record hadn't in fact been broken. Ever the gentleman, Mr Gill, then as well as now.

The mark of any decent reserve goalkeeper is to be ready when called upon. Dave Hollins hadn't waited years not to be ready. He had no time to feel any great sympathy for his unfortunate friend either. One man's loss is another man's gain, it's a dog-eat-dog world, etc. For Dave the time had come to focus and apply everything he'd learned in three years of understudying as a professional, plus whatever he'd picked up beforehand from his father and playing for Merrow. This really was it.

'I think if you asked any retired goalkeeper, or any retired player for that matter, which game stands out above all others from their career, the vast majority of them would probably say their debut,' says Dave. 'I'm no different. That's the one you remember, except that I don't actually remember that much about it! We drew 2-2 but the whole match went by in a flash. What I really recall is the feeling of how marvellous it all was, the thrill of running out on to the field in front of a big crowd for the very first time. It's not so much about the game, more that you've played first-team football at last. All the other lads in the team were wonderful and very supportive. And that's where I do start to get a bit emotional because so many of them aren't here anymore. All those fine lads, gone. There's just a couple perhaps left now, plus Eric and me. I wouldn't go as far as calling it a bittersweet memory but that element does make me sad. We are talking a long, long time ago now.'

Writing in the local *Evening Argus* newspaper, the highly respected Sussex-based sports journalist Jack Arlidge was full of praise for Dave on his big day:

> Eric turned up at Brighton station with the rest of the team but was obviously ill and returned home. This gave Hollins his big chance and there was something of a storybook flavour about the way he took it. Struggling Coventry, thrashed the previous week and with Fourth Division prospects looming up forebodingly before them, fought furiously to try and take full points from this match. Young Hollins looked remarkably free from nerves but now his goal was besieged. He threw himself sideways at several fierce shots to fingertip them to safety, soared high to deal with dangerous crosses, or went plunging into the thick mud to save at the feet of home forwards. The crowd appreciated his pluck and he received many rounds of applause. When the last long whistle

sounded and the players trudged off the muddy battleground, veteran Charlie Ashcroft, the City goalkeeper, grasped Dave's hand in congratulation and the fans raised a final cheer for him.

* * *

A 2-2 draw at Coventry, a 2-1 home win over Shrewsbury Town and a 1-1 draw away to Reading. Not a bad run for a young goalkeeper playing his first senior matches in the hurly-burly world of the Football League. Alas, once Eric had recovered from his heavy bout of flu, so Dave made way for the older, more experienced man as Brighton approached the home straight of the 1957/58 season.

The picture towards the top of the Third Division South almost inevitably became more congested as other clubs still in with a chance of promotion went for broke. When night fell on Monday, 28 April, Brighton lay third on goal difference behind Brentford and Plymouth Argyle. All three clubs were on 58 points under the two points for a win system, with Brentford and Plymouth having both completed their 46-match fixture lists. Brighton, however, still had one match left to play, a rescheduled home encounter against Watford postponed from January. Win or draw and they'd be promoted to the Promised Land of the Second Division.

The omens prior to kick-off looked good. Brighton were at full strength whereas Watford had nothing left to play for, consigned as they were to finishing in the bottom half of the table and a starting place in the new Fourth Division the following season. Only nerves, so it seemed, could throw a spanner in the works this time around.

Billy Lane's match programme notes outlined how crucial the match was:

> I should think that in the history of our club there has not been a match so important as the visit from our friends from Watford this evening. Promotion for the Albion to the Second Division rests on the result of tonight's match. It has been a strain on the players during the past few weeks but they have got over their 'tension' period and are going into tonight's match with all the fervour of the Albion boys as we know them. Tonight is the night for the ALBION ROAR and I am certain that supporters will, by their enthusiasm, prove their support for the boys by a resounding ROAR and so play a major part in giving the Albion promotion. It will not be through lack of encouragement from patrons if we unfortunately miss that coveted honour. So here's to a good, clean, sporting and entertaining match in this, the Albion's last match of the campaign.

'The ground that night was absolutely jam-packed,' recalls Eric. 'I'm pretty sure it was a record attendance for the club at that time. They were passing the kids over people's heads for them to sit on the touchline, as they used to do at the time, a good couple of hours before kick-off. Personally, I never thought we would buckle. Everything was fine-tuned to winning. We *had* to win promotion. That was all Billy Lane ever thought of – "I've got to win promotion for this club." Having come so close on so many occasions beforehand, we weren't going to pass up an opportunity like that.'

All the same, Eric made extra certain that he went through all his regular pre-match superstitions: left boot on first in the dressing room (despite being right-footed); kick the foot of both goalposts on running out on to the field; touch the crossbar. 'I don't know why I used to do the boot thing, but in 20-odd years of playing professional football I never put my right boot on first,' he says. 'It always had to be my left. Strange, isn't it? It became a habit very early on and I stuck to it. All players have things they do, little superstitions, and they were mine.'

In the end, there were no nerves. A hat-trick inside the opening ten minutes from Hove-born Adrian Thorne, just 20 years old at the time, put the result almost beyond doubt before a couple of Brighton's players had even touched the ball. It finished 6-0. Fifty-seven years after being formed in a local pub, Brighton & Hove Albion had reached the second tier of English football for the first time. Thorne, scorer of five of the six goals, was the undisputed hero of the moment, and rightly so. But Eric more than played his part on the night, plunging to his left to make an excellent save while the game was goalless. Had that gone in, well, who knows how the evening might have panned out?

Of course, by the time the final whistle sounded and the jubilant crowd had invaded the pitch, everybody had long since forgotten about Eric's crucial early intervention. Such is life for the all-too-often unsung goalkeeper.

'After the game we stayed at the club enjoying ourselves because, well, we'd done it,' says Eric. 'Normally we'd get ourselves bathed, dressed and then go home. Not for that one though. We stayed on and the crowd stayed on too, quite late into the night. They were calling for us to come out on to the pitch, which we did. And it was marvellous. We'd achieved a little bit of history. People say it was the first time Brighton won promotion to the Second Division but it was actually the first time Brighton had won promotion full stop. It had never, ever happened before. We'd achieved something no other Brighton team had done. That's got to be worth celebrating.'

'I remember it vividly,' adds Dave. 'The celebrations were unbelievable because, as Eric says, it was the first time Brighton had ever really achieved anything. The champagne was flowing everywhere in the dressing room but that's where it stopped for me and the other reserve team players. As I've already said, there was this hierarchy to the way football clubs operated then. There certainly was at Brighton, anyway. There was the first team, and there was the reserve team. I'd played for the first team by that time but I was still the reserve team's goalkeeper. The reserves were there that night as onlookers from the stands and in the dressing room. That was the discipline. Today, the entire squad at a football club would be made to feel part of an achievement like that. They'd all be involved. Not then. It was still a brilliant, wonderful, fantastic night though.'

Eccentric. Serene. Vulnerable. Brave. Intellectual. Slightly mad. Goalkeepers are all these things and much, much more. Party animals? No siree. True, there have been exceptions. The great Edwardian goalkeeper Leigh Roose, declared missing in action in 1916 at the Battle of the Somme, springs to mind for his playboy lifestyle, as does the former Australian international Mark Bosnich, whose partiality for recreational drugs kept many a tabloid journalist busy during the early noughties. However, the ravers tend to be the exceptions to the rule. There's just too much riding on a goalkeeper's position for them to drop their guard, even when off duty.

While Albion's reserve team keeper may or may not have stolen a glass of champagne – Dave can't quite remember now – he most definitely returned to his bed sober at the end of the evening. Likewise Eric, who made it as far as a restaurant that night but remained in full possession of his faculties throughout. Anyhow, he had the welfare of his guests at The Perrimay, including young Dave, to consider the following morning.

Not all Albion's first XI woke up the following day so bright-eyed and bushy-tailed, however.

'I left the ground already a bit worse for wear and went to a pub,' says Adrian Thorne. 'I was with Denis Foreman and a friend of his who had come over from South Africa and was a Catholic priest. I don't suppose he should have been drinking in pubs but it was a special occasion, so you can forgive him for that. We had a few more drinks and then it was basically up to the priest to look after the inebriated. He went round in a vehicle taking players back to their abodes, making sure they all got home safely. We had a great night, I can tell you, the kind that gives you a sore head for days.'

'As a team we didn't used to mix a lot outside the club, strangely enough, but I think that was quite common in football then,' reflects Eric. 'We were professional colleagues rather than comrades and a lot of that was down to the fact that when you were out of the first team, you didn't earn so much. Everybody was a rival to you. It really was dog eat dog. Once the pay structure changed and the restrictions on what you could earn as a footballer went out of the window, then things did become a bit more relaxed. But, at that time, we didn't do much celebrating together other than the night we won promotion and the odd club function. You'd train, or play, then go your separate ways, not head to the pub or the races or whatever.

'Dave and I were a bit different because we were friends but even then the pub wasn't really our scene. More like coffee house boys – that was us. Or the cinema. We used to get free tickets through the club for the Odeon in West Street, so we'd go there probably once a week to see whatever was on – *Ben-Hur*, *The Dam Busters* and what have you. Just show your football pass and in you'd go for nothing!'

There's an interesting, albeit tragic, mini postscript to Brighton's 1957/58 promotion story. After he'd retired as a footballer, Adrian Thorne taught science and physical education at secondary schools in and around London, including St George's Roman Catholic School in Maida Vale. On 8 December 1995, the headmaster at St George's, Philip Lawrence, was stabbed to death after intervening in a fight that had started outside the school's gates. In the moments immediately after he received his fatal injury, it was Thorne who rushed to be at the ailing man's side. 'I was with him when he was dying in the school foyer,' he remembers of a crime that shocked the whole of Britain. 'I went out to try and help the bloke, took his coat and put it under his head, mopped him down, and he was dying. Terrible.'

For absolutely no logical reason, someone within Brighton's backroom set-up had arranged for the first team to head off on a six-match tour of England's eastern counties as soon as the league season had finished. Talk about a hangover on top of a hangover.

Once the players had returned and enjoyed a much-needed break, so attentions switched to what lay ahead over the coming months. The fixture list for the 1958/59 season featured some old familiar names, clubs Albion had gone toe to toe with many times in the Third Division South, such as Leyton Orient, Ipswich Town and Bristol City. Then there were the so-called big boys such as Liverpool, Sheffield Wednesday and Sunderland, unknown quantities as far as Brighton were concerned currently residing in English football's second tier but with plenty of top-flight pedigree. Middlesbrough, their opponents on the first day of the season, Saturday, 23 August, belonged firmly in that latter category.

It was, in hindsight, always going to be a tough match. Middlesbrough had a centre-forward in their ranks who scored for fun. His name was Brian Clough. In 222 appearances for the north-eastern club spanning 1955 to 1961, Clough hit either 204 or 207 goals, depending which source you care to believe (Clough, unsurprisingly, always went for 207). Albion were at less than full strength with several key players missing, Eric among them (catching flu once in a calendar year is unfortunate but, I ask you, twice?).

Still, Dave was ready to deputise once again. And Clough, clocking a rookie in goal with the sort of relish that a coyote reserves for a roadrunner, was about to put him to the sword.

'Oh, my good god,' says Dave at the memory. 'Put it this way, after the first five or ten minutes, I don't think we had a shot at their goal. They were consistently in our half of the field. Shots were coming in from all over and we lost heavily. At times it was a struggle to get out of our 18-yard box. It was horrible, absolutely horrible.'

How heavily did Brighton lose? That would be 9-0. And, as stated in the introduction to this book, Clough scored five of them.

'I kicked off nine times and I think I touched the ball more than anybody on our side,' striker John Shepherd, who made his Brighton debut that day, recalled in 2014. 'Cloughie got all those goals, I got five or six kicks to my legs, and I don't think I even had a shot at goal. It was one of those games where you weren't in it at all. Afterwards it was a bit like, flipping heck, what's this all about? What have we let ourselves in for? Everything went right for them and nothing went right for us, but when someone single-handedly scores five goals against you, then you know he can't be bad.'

'I came up against Cloughie many times over the years and I can say that I really, really disliked playing against him,' adds Dave. 'For a goalkeeper, he was an absolute nightmare to deal with. However, tactically, he was brilliant. He controlled every Middlesbrough player on the pitch that day verbally. You do that, you do this, you go there, don't do that, and so on. He never stopped talking. He was management material even then, seeing things on the pitch other players couldn't see. The best manager that

England never had – isn't that what they call him? I can't say I disagree with that.'

'*Thank god that wasn't me*,' was Eric's reaction on hearing the scoreline from Middlesbrough's Ayresome Park, along with a huge slice of sympathy for his friend. 'Every goalkeeper has their ups and downs and Dave's had to live with that match all his life,' he says. 'Poor bloke, going in and having to suffer that. He went on to have [slight spoiler alert here] a wonderful career, so it's not as if it defined him though. Would I have done any better? I'd like to think I would but you just never know. Dave was up against Clough, who was a bit of a one-off. Maybe I dodged a bullet there!'

Dave Hollins could easily have faded into obscurity in the wake of Brighton's humiliation at the hands of Middlesbrough. He'd waited so long to make his debut in Brighton's first team. Now, in only his fourth appearance, he'd become back-page headlines for all the wrong reasons. Football is, and always has been, littered with goalkeeping casualties who were unable to bounce back from demoralising defeats early on in their careers, often because they were never given the chance. Concede nine in your fourth match and you risk becoming damaged goods. You're not Dave Hollins anymore. You're Dave 'Middlesbrough Nine' Hollins. Managers can lose faith in you. Worse still, other managers will hardly be in a rush to buy you. Suddenly your career has the life expectancy of a small boy peering into a gas tank with a lighted match.

Fortunately, Dave had a team-mate with an old head on some relatively young shoulders to provide both consolation and advice. On the train home from

Middlesbrough that evening, Dave Sexton made a point of seeking out Brighton's young goalkeeper. 'He said to me, "Forget it. It's all part and parcel of the game. You've got a long career ahead of you. You're going to be very good. Forget it and move on." And I did. Well, I never totally forgot about it, but I put that game behind me long enough to recover. Dave was a bit like a father figure to me and I will always be eternally grateful to him for taking the time to do that. He went on to reach the top of his profession as a manager and I got a glimpse there and then of how he did it. He picked me up when I needed picking up.'

Dave Sexton's pep talk would, indeed, work wonders in the long term. Short term, however, Billy Lane couldn't wait to get Eric Gill off his sick bed and back in goal for the visit of Charlton Athletic to the Goldstone Ground seven days later. Charlton possessed a battering ram of a defender called John Hewie who loved nothing better than ploughing into goalkeepers at speed, just what you need after a week in bed with flu. Eric knew all about Hewie from his own time as a young player at The Valley but, despite the physical risks and feeling less than A1, wild horses couldn't drag him from the field that day.

'I really wanted to win that one, what with it being Charlton, but we got a 2-2 draw, which was still a good result for us at the time,' says Eric. 'John Hewie was a great player, a big fella and a lovely guy. Mind you, men like him were good guys when you were playing with them but they weren't so good when you were playing against them. He spent most of the time trying to knock me into the goal. Back then, it was generally accepted that you could challenge a goalkeeper shoulder to shoulder.

What wasn't so good was when a goalkeeper went up to catch a ball and an outfield player hit them in the middle of the chest while they were in the air. That's what John Hewie would try and do. He didn't get me that day, though, so although we drew the match, I would class that as a victory!'

Hewie might not have 'got' Eric but there were several others who did over the coming months. For the first time in his career, the seemingly invincible Londoner began missing matches, largely as a consequence of coming out on the wrong end of robust challenges. At the time, he dismissed such traumas as part and parcel of the game. Today, while discussing the riskier elements of goalkeeping in the 1950s, Eric does so with a shrug of the shoulders, shorthand for 'it happened'. However, knowing what we now know about footballers suffering from neurodegenerative diseases later in life, listening to him talk about the physical damage he incurred over the course of 1958 and 1959 is enough to make the hairs on the back of your neck stand up.

'It's funny, but a lot of this I'd kind of blanked out, or just forgotten, until now,' admits Eric. 'I ended up in hospital a lot. There were times when you got challenged when you were going up for the ball in the air, but there were other things as well. On one occasion, I got this kick in the head. I dived for the ball. He – I couldn't tell you who it was – took a swing at it with his boot and he caught me full on. I was unconscious. I don't know how long for. Afterwards they told me to go home, go to bed and not to move. We had a club doctor but most of the medical stuff was left to the trainer, Joe Wilson, who would come

on to the pitch and see to us. Lovely guy that he was, Joe
wasn't a medic. It was just the old bucket and a sponge to
try and bring you round. Anyway, it was obviously pretty
serious because I did eventually end up in hospital. I really
wasn't right at all. A bucket and sponge isn't going to do
the trick when you're unconscious, is it?'

Today, goalkeepers are generally regarded as being
over-protected creatures. Listening to Eric, or reading
through old newspaper reports, you begin to understand
why that might be the case. The death of Celtic's John
Thomson in September 1931 hours after his head had come
into contact with an opponent's knee in a match against
their Glasgow rivals Rangers remains a relatively well-
documented goalkeeping fatality. But there were others,
many others in fact. Take James Utterson, for example,
who died as a consequence of being kicked over the heart
while playing in a reserve-team match for Wolverhampton
Wanderers. Or Sunderland's Jimmy Thorpe, roughed up
to such an extent while playing against Chelsea that he
suffered a recurrence of a diabetic condition that had lain
dormant in his body for two years, causing him to die in
hospital five days later.

Then there were all the near-misses, hundreds (if
not thousands) of them over the decades, the most
high-profile of all coming in the 1956 FA Cup Final at
Wembley Stadium when the thigh of Birmingham City's
Peter Murphy collided with the neck of Manchester City
goalkeeper Bert Trautmann. Once again, the bucket
and sponge were in attendance. Once again, they were
no help whatsoever to a man rendered unconscious and
requiring urgent medical attention. Despite only being

able to see silhouettes and in what he later described as 'absolute agony', Trautmann played on for the 17 minutes that remained, making several saves in the process. Three days later what initially had been dismissed as a crick in the neck was found in fact to be a broken neck. Trautmann could have been paralysed or died at any point.

Two years after that a sizeable television audience witnessed Bolton's Nat Lofthouse smash Manchester United goalkeeper Harry Gregg, complete with ball, over the line at Wembley in what remains one of the most controversial moments in FA Cup history. At that point the powers that be, conscious perhaps that the death of a goalkeeper on live TV might not portray the game in its best light, seemed to decide enough was enough. From that point on goalkeepers were afforded increasing levels of protection. 'I only wish it had always been like it is now,' adds Eric ruefully. 'Then we'd have been able to do our jobs properly.'

Eric's injury-enforced absences at least provided Dave with opportunities to redeem himself following the Middlesbrough debacle of August 1958. Over the course of the 1958/59 campaign Eric appeared in 27 of Brighton's 42 league matches, with Dave making up the remaining 15 (plus one additional outing in an FA Cup defeat to Bradford City). Bottom of the Second Division in early September, Brighton improved steadily over the months that followed to finish the season comfortably in mid-table, playing entertaining football in front of large, adoring crowds, the kind of attendances Billy Lane always sensed would materialise if the club could only achieve a measure of relative success.

There was still the odd hiccup along the way, mind. On Saturday, 20 December 1958, Middlesbrough made the long trip south to the Goldstone Ground to play the return fixture. This time it was Eric's turn to face and be tormented by Brian Clough. The match proved to be an absolute corker for any neutrals in the crowd with Middlesbrough prevailing 6-4, Clough scoring three times to take his season's tally against Brighton to eight goals in two matches.

However, it was more than just Clough's sharp-shooting that undid Eric.

'Clough relied a lot on intimidation,' declares Eric. 'He'd run into you, but it was unlike other centre-forwards might run into you. It was more subtle. Back then, when a goalkeeper had the ball in their hands, centre-forwards would often stand in front of them to harass them. Clough did it more than anybody else. He'd try little things to get you to mess up. When you moved, he'd move, sometimes bumping into you.

'He would chase goalkeepers all over the place and, on that occasion, he kicked me in the knee. And before you ask, yes, it was deliberate. He was trying to intimidate me and that was part of his way of doing it. He was a wonderful player, though, Clough, no doubt about that. He was a class act.'

Clough may have won the battles that season but Brighton ultimately won the war. Once all the fixtures had been played and the points were in, Middlesbrough somehow conspired to finish below Brighton in the Second Division table, despite beating them 15-4 over the course of two matches.

As Clough himself once quipped about his own philosophy on life, 'If you don't laugh, you cry.'

Footnote: there has been some conjecture over the years as to whether Eric Gill and Ted Ditchburn did in fact break a Football League record for goalkeepers with their shared tally of 247 consecutive matches played (records, so it seem, aren't made to be broken but to be argued about endlessly). For the purposes of this book, I have gone with what all major news organisations, including the BBC, reported at the time and that the majority of sources, so it seems, still believe to be correct. No matter what, the record was subsequently broken by the late Ray Clemence who, between 1972 and 1978, played 336 back-to-back matches in goal for Liverpool, a tally that's unlikely to be broken in the modern era of squad rotation, if indeed ever. Harold Bell, a centre-half with Tranmere Rovers during the 1940s and 50s, holds the Football League record for consecutive appearances covering all positions, having played 429, 446 or 461 on the trot, again depending which source you choose to go with.

6

SUMMERTIME BLUES

*'The ultimate measure of a man is not where he
stands in moments of comfort and convenience,
but where he stands at times of challenge and
controversy.'* – Martin Luther King Jr

ONE MORNING in November 1959, Billy Lane sent
word to Dave Hollins that he wanted to see him in his
office at the Goldstone Ground pronto. Dave had never
been summoned in such a manner by his boss before but
common sense told him this was going to be a pressing
piece of either good or bad news. He certainly wasn't
expecting a lesson of sorts in his family tree.

'I'd grown up in Guildford,' says Dave. 'Until I came
to Brighton that was pretty much all I knew. Guildford
born and bred ... or so I thought. Anyway, Billy Lane
calls me into his office and says he's got wonderful news
for me. I'd only just started playing regularly for the first
team. I thought, *Crikey, I can't be on the move already.* Billy
says, "Congratulations, you've been selected to play for
the Welsh under-23s against Scotland." And I sat back

and thought, *How can this be?* It turned out that I was Guildford raised but Bangor, as in North Wales, born. My father, who you'll remember was also a goalkeeper, had finished his playing career with Bangor City in the Welsh League and that's where I'd been born, something I was totally and utterly unaware of. That qualified me to play for Wales. I just couldn't believe it … but in a nice way.'

Two weeks later, on Wednesday, 25 November, Dave found himself warming up in front of a respectable five-figure crowd at the Racecourse Ground, Wrexham, ready to start against a Scottish team featuring the young Denis Law, already the subject of intense transfer speculation involving Manchester City, Manchester United and Liverpool. Four months later City would win the race for the centre-forward's signature, splashing out a then British record transfer fee of £55,000 to bring him from Huddersfield Town. On the night in question, Dave and his defenders kept Law, who'd already made his full Scotland debut, remarkably quiet in the torrential North Wales rain.

Far more of a problem was Law's strike partner, young John White of Tottenham Hotspur. Time and time again White, who would tragically be killed by lightning aged just 27 while out on a Middlesex golf course, had the Welsh goal in his sights. Time and time again Dave denied him with outstanding saves. When White did finally manage to put the ball in the net, the goal was disallowed for a push, ensuring the contest finished all square at 1-1.

'That match was a turning point for me, and not just because it was when I realised I had Welsh connections,' reflects Dave. 'The players who I was playing against were big names. Something inside you says, *This is it – I think I've made it.* Of course, you don't want to get too far ahead of yourself, but that's the reaction you have. John White and Denis Law were already stars, so to keep them off the scoresheet that night was quite an achievement. It's like when you meet a pop star or a big personality and, after a while with them, you start to think, *Well, they're only normal people.* You realise that, deep down, they are no different to you. That's quite important psychologically when you're a goalkeeper. The last thing you want to feel is intimidated. Instead, you start to look at yourself as an equal.'

Off the field, Dave's life was starting to change in other ways too. One morning during the Easter weekend of 1957 he'd been out walking along the Brighton seafront with Norman Stevens, an Albion fringe player, when their paths conveniently crossed with two young ladies called Jackie and Christine. Straight off, Dave felt a connection with Jackie. He asked her out on a date. She accepted. As first dates go, well, let's just say Dave was more the Invisible Man than Cary Grant.

'He arranged to meet me in Brighton down by The Pavilion,' recalls Jackie. 'The plan was to go from there to, I think, the pictures. So I went down to meet him and I stood there, and I stood there, and I stood there … and nothing happened. Then, all of a sudden, this chap called Don Bates comes along. Don used to play cricket for Sussex. Why it was Don who brought the message, I don't know, but he said Dave had sent him to tell me that he'd had to go and play football. Instead of standing me up, he'd sent Don to say he was sorry and we'd get together another time, which I actually thought was rather nice.'

With Dave's football commitments and National Service impending, getting together was always going to be an issue for the two teenagers. However, a relationship of sorts began that very nearly hit the buffers after Dave joined up with the Royal Army Medical Corps.

'I basically saw him when he was on leave, which was also when he had to squeeze his football in, so there wasn't much time for us at all,' says Jackie. 'That was the trouble really. He didn't want me going out anywhere else and got a little bit possessive. Being young, I thought, *Oh gosh, I'm not having this*, and called it a day with him. After that we didn't see each other for maybe two years while he finished doing his National Service. Then one day I was at a Brighton Tigers game, the ice hockey team who were quite big at the time, with my friends. Brighton & Hove Albion always had a box at the stadium and, on that particular occasion, he was there. And I thought, *Umm, I do like him really!* And it just went from there.'

Dave and Jackie got married at St Andrew's Church in Moulsecoomb, Brighton, when he was 22 and she was 19, an occasion that, among other things, brought the curtain down on his time lodging with Eric and Ida at The Perrimay in Charlotte Street.

'That had been Dave's home, so we spent quite a lot of time there when we got together,' adds Jackie, who worked in the offices of Southdown Motor Services, the local bus and coach operator, on £2 5s. a week. 'They were a wonderful couple. Ida had been like a mum to him. She always said that Dave was like a third son. There was a bond there that never went away. So off we went and got married and moved into an apartment owned by the football club up by Brighton train station.'

For Dave to be like a third son, Eric and Ida must clearly have been busy in other departments. Besides being a professional footballer and overseeing the running of a business, Eric was now the proud father of two boys, Steve and Malcolm (who Dave and Jackie often babysat, allowing Eric and Ida to enjoy some much-needed downtime together). It should have been the happiest time of his life. And as befits a kid of the Blitz given to putting life's little jolts into perspective, it was. But it would have been a lot happier had Billy Lane not welcomed in the 1960s by seeming to go out of his way to sabotage Eric's career as a goalkeeper.

The 1959/60 season had begun well for Eric, given the nod by Lane to start ahead of Dave in Brighton's first team. After losing their opening two league fixtures, the team settled down and recorded some impressive wins – most notably a handsome 3-1 victory over south coast rivals Portsmouth – to sit comfortably in mid-table after eight matches.

Then, at home against Plymouth Argyle on Saturday, 19 September, Eric received another kick to the head, opening the door once again for Dave to come in and prove his worth. Which he duly did. Away to Liverpool in mid-October, Dave turned in a towering performance to help secure a 2-2 draw, saving a second-half penalty at Anfield's Kop end taken by Jimmy Melia (who in 1983 would walk out as Brighton's manager at Wembley Stadium in the FA Cup Final). Watching from the stands,

SUMMERTIME BLUES

Wales's selectors were more than a little impressed, hence the call to represent the under-23s against Scotland the following month.

From that point on, Dave's stock soared. Consigned to the reserves, Eric, back to full fitness by mid-November, could only watch as his close friend ran with Brighton's goalkeeping baton. Even so, no one, least of all Eric, could have foreseen what lay in store in May 1960 once the club had secured its Second Division berth for another season by finishing a solid if unspectacular 14th in the table.

'There was a shop across the road from the Goldstone Ground, which we used to nip in to get the papers and read all about the games, seeing if our names were in there,' remembers Eric. 'One day one of the lads – and I can't remember who it was – must have nipped in there and seen the headlines. He comes back and says, "I think you should get the *Argus* today, Eric." I said "Why?" He says, "Well go and get one and you'll see." So, I went and bought one and there it was plastered right across the page – "Record breaker Gill on the transfer list". I couldn't believe it. Billy Lane didn't even have the decency to call me into his office and tell me. I had to read it in the newspaper. I thought, *Well that's nice, isn't it?* He never said a word to me. Not one.'

Over the days that followed, Eric's relationship with Billy Lane unravelled at pace. In 1960, the wages received by players, together with the terms of their contracts, were akin, to quote Eric, to 'making us slaves'. And he was far, far from alone in subscribing to that belief. The maximum wage remained in force, restricting players to no more than £20 per week during the season and £17 in the summer (although many received substantially less). In addition, players weren't simply allowed to move when their contracts expired, something that potentially tied them to one club for life. It was, in short, an archaic system, one that amounted to a colossal restraint of one's trade.

'If a club didn't want you, they could put you on the transfer list but keep your registration, which is what happened to me in the end at Brighton,' says Eric. 'So long as they kept your registration, you couldn't go anywhere else. All the cards were stacked in their favour. I know it's a strong word, but we were slaves. All you could get in those days was a one-year contract. When that year ran out, that was the end of your wages, unless they offered you another year. That's how clubs behaved back then, or how they could behave. And some of them, if your manager was a rotten sod, did.'

Off his own bat, Eric discovered Bristol City were keen to sign him on the free transfer that, being out of contract, he was perfectly entitled to. He travelled to the west country, met their manager, liked what City had to say and was ready to sign on the dotted line. All that remained was for Brighton to agree to surrender Eric's registration form by way of a telephone call.

'Bristol City said, "We've got Eric Gill here, we want to sign him, can you do the necessities." And that should have been that,' Eric recalls. 'Then Billy Lane comes on the line and says, "In that case the fee is £2,000," which was quite a bit of money in those days. So, their manager says, "I'm sorry Eric, no go. I'm not doing business with a man like that, someone who gives you a free transfer and then puts a price on your head." If Billy Lane didn't want me, why wouldn't he let me play for someone who did? Because he was frightened I'd go to another club and make a success of it, that's why. Then people would've turned round and said, "Why on earth did you let him go?" I'd given him eight years' service and that's the way he chose to repay me. It was all a bit vicious. And he was a vicious bugger, Billy Lane.'

Amid all the rancour, salvation of sorts raised its head in the shape of Guildford City, who by that stage had designs on climbing the ladder and being elected to the Football League. Besides being relatively local to Brighton, Guildford City were willing to pay Eric more or less what he'd been on in wages at the Goldstone Ground. Crucially, there was also no way that Brighton & Hove Albion nor Billy Lane could block the move as rules governing the registration of players only applied to clubs in the Football League.

'They were a lovely club, Guildford City, they really were,' says Eric. 'They had a board of directors who were so enthusiastic and ploughed quite a lot of money into it simply because they loved the club. They were in the second tier of the Southern League at the time, so we're talking non-league football, but I really had no alternative, given the way Billy Lane was behaving, if I wanted to carry on playing. They were a club that wanted to go places, though, and got pretty big crowds. Their manager was a guy called Albert Tennant, who'd been a coach at Chelsea. All the players got on well with him. They had the pick of the best players who were coming out of the Football League because they had a bit of money behind them. In fact, quite a few of the lads I'd been with at Brighton, including Dennis Gordon and Albert Mundy, ended up coming with me to Guildford.'

Eric's departure from the Goldstone Ground that summer left a sour taste in the mouths of his ex-team-mates and supporters. The former were accustomed, given the lack of job security, to being treated like cattle. Even so, letting a club record breaker leave at the relatively young age of 29 seemed a somewhat bizarre decision, even accounting for Dave's emergence as a goalkeeper of real quality.

Above all, it was the heartless manner in which Eric was cast adrift that jarred. The extent of the breakdown in relationship between Eric and Billy Lane went unreported in the press. That didn't stop fans writing in their droves to local newspapers and indeed Brighton & Hove Albion expressing disappointment at Eric's sudden exit. He had, after all, become, in the words of the *Evening Argus*, 'one of, if not the, most popular sportsmen in Sussex'.

Nevertheless, football was, and continues to be, a game of short memories, where the seemingly irreplaceable of today can be shown the door faster than it takes to write the word tomorrow as the circus rolls ever onwards. By August 1960, Eric was commuting from Brighton to Guildford in his stylish Ford Zephyr ('one of those with the bench seats in the front – I could fly about a bit in that') for training on Tuesday and Thursday evenings, and to wherever the club happened to be playing on Saturdays.

In January 1961, after years of arguments, the Professional Footballers' Association (PFA), the union that serves to protect, improve and negotiate the conditions, rights and status of professional players in England and Wales, succeeded under its chairman Jimmy Hill in having the maximum wage abolished. However, the Football League refused to budge on the wider issues involving contracts. In response, the PFA declared strike action, beginning with all matches scheduled to be played on Saturday, 21 January. With public and media support building behind the players' cause, the Football League climbed down, agreeing to abolish antiquated regulations that, in effect, tied footballers to one club for life.

If Eric had only been transfer-listed by Billy Lane a matter of months later he would have been free to sign for any other club in the Football League that wanted him.

* * *

It might have been George Harrison who spoke the immortal words. Or Dennis Hopper. Or maybe Grace Slick or Paul Kantner of the band Jefferson Airplane. Either way, whoever said, 'If you remember the 60s, you weren't there,' sure as hell wasn't an overworked, slightly battered goalkeeper. Switched on – most certainly. Turn on, tune in, drop out – never in a million years.

The 60s remain seared into the memory of Dave Hollins. The vast majority of those memories, it has to be said, are good ones. But Eric's exit, right at the beginning of the decade, hit him hard. His friend still lived and indeed worked locally, so it wasn't as though the pair didn't see each other regularly. However, when you're used to having someone around the workplace, a mentor, and that person moves on (in the sourest of circumstances), then it's going to create a gigantic hole.

'Eric was part of the furniture at the Albion,' says Dave. 'He'd played so many consecutive games, been there so many years and been such a presence in my and other people's lives. Then, all of a sudden, he was gone. I was still quite young at the time, so becoming the outright first-team goalkeeper was quite a responsibility, a bit like learning to ride a bicycle without any stabilisers. You've got to go it alone. I was ready by then but, yes, I missed having him around on a day-to-day basis.'

Still, with Eric gone, Dave could now focus on stringing together a long unbroken run of his own in Brighton's first team. Or so he thought.

In October 1960, Billy Lane opted to field reserve-team goalkeeper Charlie Baker, a semi-professional player not long out of National Service, away to Notts County in the club's first-ever appearance in the inaugural League Cup competition. Dave wasn't overly concerned, assuming he'd be back between the posts for the league match at Sheffield United the following Saturday. Except he wasn't. Before long, Charlie was starting more matches in the first team than Dave.

'I felt really guilty about it,' says Charlie, still very much alive and living in Sussex, of the situation he suddenly found himself him. 'Dave was a Wales under-23 international and I worked in precision engineering, playing for Brighton on a semi-professional contract. It didn't seem right somehow. I made my debut in the League Cup at Notts County and thought that was that, at least for the time being. Then Billy Lane says, "You're stopping on and playing against Sheffield United at Bramall Lane on Saturday."

Even though we lost 2-1, it seemed I did enough to stay in the side from then on.'

'Charlie was a local lad, a nice lad, who I'd done a little bit to nurture,' recalls Dave. 'I thought, *Well, if he asks me questions, then I'll answer them.* So, we got on okay. Then Charlie starts playing in the first team. I thought, *What's going on here then?* He was a promising young goalkeeper, don't get me wrong, but I'd worked hard and waited a long time to get hold of that jersey. Then the penny dropped – Billy Lane was banking on the fact he would sell me. He wanted to protect what he saw as an asset and play me only in certain games. "Putting you in the shop window" was the terminology they used. By playing Charlie, he was testing him to see if he could become his first-team goalkeeper in my absence, which is quite clever really.'

'I'd read in the *Argus* that there was talk of Dave being sold,' adds Charlie. 'One week Billy Lane said to me, "I'm going to leave you out on Saturday. Somebody wants to take a look at Dave." I thought, *That's fair enough, I don't mind*, because there am I, still feeling a bit guilty about what's going on. Everybody wanted to be in the first team as you'd be on better money, but I was quite happy to stand aside. The following week Billy said he'd bring me back to play at Sunderland. I arrived at King's Cross station in London, as I'd arranged, to meet the rest of the team to catch the train up to the north-east, and who should be standing on the platform but Dave! I thought to myself, *Maybe I'm not playing after all.* It was only once the train got going that I worked out what was happening.'

What was happening was this. For some considerable months, several clubs, Newcastle United and Everton among them, had indeed been tracking Dave. The Wednesday prior to Brighton's match at Sunderland, 15 March 1961, Newcastle had tabled a sizeable bid (for the times, and for a goalkeeper) of £11,000 (£270,000 in 2022 values). United vice-chairman Stanley Seymour (who'd played for and managed the club, hence his nickname of 'Mr Newcastle United') had watched Dave in the flesh and decided he was worth it. Brighton were in no place to stand in Dave's way. Nor did they want to, given the amount of money involved. The deal was completed later that same day.

Now Dave was on the train heading north to meet his new team-mates who, without a match that day and by sheer coincidence, were due to attend the Sunderland versus Brighton match as guests.

'Back then, even though things were starting to change, players still had very little control over anything,' says Dave. 'Whatever the manager said, you did. I got on fine with Billy Lane. The thing is, he was the boss. There's a barrier, and you had respect for that. He could be a ruthless bastard though. I didn't have many dealings with him anyway, at least not financially. If you had to deal with him financially, as Eric did at the end, then you were in trouble. When Newcastle came in for me, the first I knew about it was when he called me into his office and said, "We're going up to London." I said, "We are?" He said, "Newcastle have come in for you. Stan Seymour's been watching you and they've put in a bid, which we've agreed." And off to London we went to meet the Newcastle delegation in a hotel at King's Cross, where I signed on the dotted line. To be honest, I was really excited. I'd loved it at Brighton but this was Newcastle, a

First Division club with such an amazing history. They'd had all these incredible players like Jackie Milburn, who'd not long since retired. The only people I had time to tell were my wife and my dad – it all happened so fast. I remember Jackie saying, "That's a bit of a long way, isn't it?" And to be fair, it was!'

'At first it seemed like a big wrench, especially as I was expecting our first child at the time,' remembers Jackie. 'I was born in Lincolnshire but we'd moved to Brighton when I was about seven years old. I'd grown up there, got a job there, got married there. But the more I thought about it, the more I was all for it. It became like this adventure, the start of a new life together. It was his career as well, and we were both excited that he was going to a club like Newcastle. By the time we actually came to move, I was taking it all in my stride.'

It was only years later, well after his playing career had finished, that Dave got to realise the extent of the interest that had existed in him during those final months at Brighton, particularly from Everton.

'After his own playing career had finished, my brother John managed Chelsea and I used to go up quite regularly to Stamford Bridge to watch them,' Dave recollects. 'This would have been in the 80s. One day I was going through the main gate and who should I bump into than Billy Lane. So, we got talking, discussing the game we were about to see and what have you, and then, somehow, we got on to when I'd left Brighton. And he said, "Of course, David, at the time of you going to Newcastle, you could have gone to Everton. I could have sent you there, but I chose Newcastle." And I thought to myself, *Well he didn't tell me that!* But, in those days, you weren't told anything. There were no agents or other interested parties. You were told things on a need-to-know basis. If you were going to be transferred, then it was entirely up to your manager where you went. Would it have made any difference, knowing I could've gone to Everton instead? I don't think so. I was brought up in a footballing family and, to me, it didn't matter where I went or who I played for. As I've already said, it was the honour. Money didn't come into it. The main thing was that you'd achieved your ambitions. That's what dad wanted for us. It was all about the honour.'

7

OUR FRIENDS IN THE NORTH

'Football is not really about winning, or goals,
or saves, or supporters. It's about glory. It's
about doing things in style, doing them with a
flourish. It's about going out to beat the other
lot, not waiting for them to die of boredom.
It's about dreaming of the glory that the double
brought.' – Danny Blanchflower

THE 'DOUBLE', so they said, couldn't be done. Many
a club had come close, only to fall at the final hurdle.
Winning the old First Division together with the FA Cup
in the same season was, it appeared, right up there with
handcuffing lightning. And only Muhammad Ali – or
Cassius Clay as he was known back in 1961 – could do
that.

Danny Blanchflower, captain of Tottenham Hotspur,
reckoned otherwise. 'It's going to be done,' he told
Wolverhampton Wanderers manager Stan Cullis, another
whose teams had come close but no cigar in 1958. 'And
Spurs will be the team to do it.'

By late March 1961, under the stewardship of manager Bill Nicholson, it looked as if Blanchflower might just be proved right. Having disposed of Burnley 3-0 in the FA Cup semi-final, all attention at White Hart Lane turned to the league where, after dropping only one point from their first 16 matches, it seemed only a miracle, or the aforementioned Cassius Clay, could halt Tottenham's progress. In the event, the miracle worker turned out to be Dave Hollins.

Five days after defeating Burnley, Tottenham entertained Newcastle United at home in what would be Dave's debut for his new employers. Newcastle may have been, to use Dave's words, 'a First Division club with such an amazing history' but their status in English football's top flight was in jeopardy. Leaking goals at an alarming rate (one of the reasons, no doubt, behind Dave's transfer), Jackie Milburn's former club were fighting a losing battle against gravity like some doomed Lancaster bomber in a Second World War movie. Could Dave be the man to pull them out of their inexorable dive? Time would tell, except that time wasn't something Newcastle particularly had in spades.

'I went up by train from Brighton the day before the game to meet the rest of the team in a big hotel by King's Cross station that Newcastle often used to stay in when we played in London,' Dave recollects. 'There were a couple of other players who, like me, had been bought close to the transfer deadline day. You had Jimmy Harrower, a striker who'd come from Liverpool, and big John McGrath, a centre-half who played a lot of games later on for Southampton. We were going into a side that was leaking goals but still had some good players like Ivor Allchurch, the Welsh international. I don't think Spurs had been beaten at home that season. I remember going out for the warm-up and the place was massive, huge. That's when I used to go into my own little world. Actually, I used to do that as soon as I arrived at a ground. It's a really strange feeling to explain to people, but you just switch off to everything that's around you apart from the game. The adrenalin starts to flow and all you are thinking about is the ball. When you're a goalkeeper, the ball can make you look like a total idiot, so you keep your eye on it all the time. Even when it goes out of play, you watch the ball. That's something my dad taught me – "Son, whatever you do, always watch the ball" – and he was right. That's sound advice, the kind I'd give any goalkeeper today.'

Occasionally in tennis you'll hear a player make a comment about how the balls in a match seemed as big as grapefruits, or watermelons, or some other type of large fruit. What they're trying to convey is how 'in the zone' they felt, as if blessed by a *Matrix*-like superpower whereby time slows down or stops altogether, enabling them to comfortably make their shots. The same principle can apply to the art of goalkeeping. Sometimes there are matches when a keeper senses that whatever the opposition throws at him or her, they'll see it coming in time to make a save. For Dave, one such occasion was White Hart Lane, Wednesday, 22 March 1961.

'It was the most wonderful game I'd ever had,' he recalls. 'Everything came off.' Well, almost everything. Spurs did in fact take a 1-0 lead in the 40th minute but, other than that, no matter what came Dave's way, he dealt with it. Twice Newcastle scored in the second half through Allchurch and Albert Scanlon to secure the most unexpected of victories, boosting their chances of First Division survival in the process.

Blanchflower may have talked about the importance of doing things in style but, in defeat, Tottenham's mask slipped somewhat.

'We had a player playing for us that day called Len White who was a prolific goalscorer,' says Dave. 'Dave Mackay, who was a hard player, was picking Len up. We were giving them a real match, which they might not have been expecting, and Dave went straight across Len and broke his leg. You could hear the noise of it going above the crowd and the whole place went really quiet. In those days there was a lot of physicality but that was a very, very nasty tackle, one that pretty much finished Len's career. He was never the same player again. It was a sickening thing, it really was, and is always in the back of my mind when I think of that game.'

Dave's definitive grapefruit/watermelon/whatever your choice of large fruit moment that evening came just before half-time when Spurs were presented with a golden opportunity to double their lead from the penalty spot.

'I'd seen Danny Blanchflower take penalties on television, so I was pretty confident that I knew where he was going to put it,' Dave confides. 'He always seemed to go for the same corner, which was to my left-hand side, so I gave him quite a bit of space to shoot at, letting him think, well, if he's giving me all that room, I'll aim there. And he did. As he was striking the ball, with his head down, just when he couldn't see what I was doing, I moved along the line. He struck it and I stopped it. I very nearly caught it actually but ended up pushing it away.'

'Stunning setback for Tottenham – robbed of two league points by Newcastle keeper'. So went the headline in *The Times* the following day. 'Tottenham, now only four points clear of Sheffield Wednesday at the head of the First Division, were thwarted by a remarkable display from Hollins, the former Brighton goalkeeper, playing his first game for Newcastle', the match report continued. 'They now approach their meridian at Wembley on May 6 with dented prestige and decidedly less certainty of achieving the league championship'.

For what it's worth, Tottenham did go on to do the 'double', beating Leicester City 2-0 at Wembley Stadium in the FA Cup Final and clinching the league title with three matches in hand. Newcastle, however, still had, if not a mountain, then a very steep hill to climb if they were going to stay in the First Division, despite their 2-1 victory.

As far as Dave was concerned, that could wait a day or two. First, he needed to find a place to live in the north-east of England for himself and his pregnant wife.

* * *

The Newcastle upon Tyne that Dave and Jackie discovered in March 1961 was a far cry from the Newcastle of today with its fancy restaurants, roaring nightlife and numerous tourist attractions. In 1961 the old established industries on which the city and its surrounding areas were built had yet to die. Grime, poverty and decay were rife. The Tyne was still a working river, as polluted as any third-world watercourse. Downstream mighty vessels rose from the ground at the Swan Hunter shipbuilding yard to tower over the surrounding streets before slipping away to explore the seas. The Animals, to paraphrase the title of one of their most popular songs, still had to get out of the place.

'I had never witnessed misery like this in my own country,' actor Michael Caine remarked on visiting Newcastle in 1970 to make the film *Get Carter*. 'It was like Charles Dickens meets Emily Brontë written by Edgar Wallace.'

And yet, despite its social issues, the place had a heart the size of those hulks built by the men of Swan Hunter.

'The club had a house about ten minutes from the ground on a street called Powburn Gardens, number 15 it was, which Bob Stokoe, who would go on to manage Sunderland but who'd been playing for Newcastle, had just vacated,' says Dave. 'We managed to get hold of that. I moved in and Jackie came up on the milk train, which was what we used to call the overnight trains, to join me. All the neighbours were so friendly. Down south you might think they were busy in a nosey way – but they weren't. They just wanted to get to know you and help. When all the furniture arrived several of them asked us into their houses to have a cup of tea. If you went out anywhere for a bite to eat, straight away people would talk to you. Everyone seemed so warm.

'Years later, probably in the 80s or maybe 90s, Jackie and I went up to Scotland and decided to stop off in Newcastle on the way home to see where we used to live. Jackie said she'd like to visit the local shops, and she was gone about half an hour. When she came back, she had tears in her eyes. I said, "What's up?" She said, "It's unbelievable – they called me Mrs Hollins." That's the quality of the people up there.'

'We couldn't have gone to a better place really,' Jackie concurs. 'We went from living in a flat in Brighton to a lovely semi-detached three-bedroom house, rented at a very nominal fee. In those days you didn't think about buying houses at our age, not even on a footballer's salary. To me, it seemed luxurious. Our eldest daughter, Angela, arrived not long after we moved in. That was a bit of a culture shock though. I wanted to have her in hospital but was told, "You're young, you're healthy, you've got the facilities at home, you can have the baby at home." I thought, *Oh my goodness me, I can't do that*, because my family were hundreds of miles away. So we found out about this place in Newcastle called the Hopedean, which was run by the Salvation Army. We paid to go there and the money from the paying guests subsidised unmarried mothers from the area who stayed for so many weeks before their due date until whenever they were ready to leave afterwards. It all seemed very primitive but somehow it worked. Our second daughter, Julie, was also born there. After she'd arrived, we gave the pram to the Salvation Army for other mothers to use.'

There weren't many football clubs in England or Wales that could touch Newcastle United during the early 1950s. The First Division title may have remained elusive but in the FA Cup the Magpies, spearheaded by their talismanic England international centre-forward Jackie Milburn, remained almost peerless. Three times in five years (1951, 1952 and 1955) the team returned to

Newcastle Central railway station trophy in hand before parading it through the city's streets in front of their adoring public. Success, so it seemed, was inherent and would go on forever.

By the time the 33-year-old Milburn pulled the plug on his first-class career to become player-manager of Belfast-based Linfield in 1957, Newcastle were already slipping into reverse gear. In the wake of their 1955 FA Cup triumph, the club had for whatever reason chosen to abolish the position of manager and revert to the old committee system of doing things, common in the pre-Second World War era but virtually redundant by that time in the professional game. With football in the UK modernising following Hungary's wake-up calls of 1953 and 1954 (the latter an even more emphatic 7-1 win over England in Budapest), decision-making by committee over something as fundamental as team selection simply wasn't going to work.

In 1957/58 Newcastle avoided relegation to the Second Division on goal average (the number of goals scored divided by the number of goals conceded), finishing 19th, having trailed in 17th place the previous season. The writing was most definitely on the wall. It's just that nobody could read what it said yet.

In June 1958, conscious that something had to change, the club flipped back to the modern era by appointing a full-time manager in the shape of Charlie Mitten, something of a nonconformist with a penchant for the limelight. Results subsequently improved as Mitten's fresh attitude and novel (for the time) training techniques paid off. However, in-fighting at boardroom level continued to detract from matters on the field as former Newcastle player, manager and chairman Stanley Seymour, still a considerable presence behind the scenes, clashed with the club's new chairman William McKeag. Rebel shareholders and well-meaning pressure groups only succeeded in fuelling the inferno. As the exasperated Mitten would later declare, 'Trying to manage the team and restructure the club was almost impossible because of the warring factions on the board.'

Still, as long as Len White carried on banging in the goals, Newcastle at least had a chance of entertaining their fans and staving off the spectre of relegation. The diminutive No. 9 with the stocky frame had already scored 29 league and cup goals during the 1960/61 campaign when Dave Mackay cut him down with that reckless, airborne assault from behind at White Hart Lane, ending White's days as a top-flight striker. If Newcastle were going to beat the drop, then they were going to have to do it without their principal asset, rated by some to be every bit as good a striker as Milburn.

Three days after upsetting Tottenham's apple cart, Dave Hollins made his home debut for Newcastle at St James' Park against a Chelsea team boasting another prolific striker – Jimmy Greaves. If there was one player any team with defensive frailties didn't want to come up against in 1961, then it was Greaves. 'He would find space where no one else would,' Martin Chivers, who played alongside Greaves at Tottenham, once remarked. 'He was like a magnet. The ball invariably found him in the area.' And, more often than not, the ball then tended to find the net, or at least the target.

That afternoon at St James' Park, Greaves dispatched the ball past Hollins into Newcastle's net no fewer than four times as Chelsea ran out 6-1 winners, all seven goals coming in a remarkable second half. Talk about coming back down to earth with a bump after the adrenalin rush of White Hart Lane the previous Wednesday evening.

'Chelsea had a huge, very talented lad up front called Ron Tindall,' remembers Dave. 'Jimmy was feeding off him. The ball would come up to Ron, he'd lay it off with his feet or head to Jimmy, and then Jimmy had all the space in the world to get his shots off. And boy, did he get his shots off – bang, bang, bang. bang! I was so exposed. It was a tremendous performance by him but Ron deserved a lot of the credit because of the way he fed him. He was one of the most fantastic goalscorers ever, Jimmy, without a doubt. It was at times like that when I applied the advice Dave Sexton had given me after that Brighton game against Middlesbrough when Cloughie scored all those goals – "forget it, it's all part and parcel of the game, move on". There's another match to be played around the corner. Your job is to focus on that.'

Dave did all he could over the ensuing seven matches to keep Newcastle in the top flight. Bereft of defensive cover in front of him and with no one on hand to score the necessary goals at the other end of the pitch, his efforts were in vain, the decisive blow coming in a 2-1 defeat away to relegation rivals Blackpool on 15 April. Home wins against Bolton Wanderers and Blackburn Rovers in their last two matches proved too little, too late. Having conceded a thumping 109 league goals over the course of the 1960/61 season, Newcastle were destined to play Second Division football for the first time since 1947.

'The damage had already been done before I arrived,' says Dave at the memory of experiencing relegation so soon after arriving on Tyneside. 'Newcastle were a big club that had been allowed to drift and make some funny decisions. Take Ronnie Simpson, for instance, who I was signed to replace, very much the same type of goalkeeper as me in an acrobatic sense. Ronnie was never finished, like they thought he was, and proved that by going to Celtic where he won a European Cup winners' medal [in 1967]. Why get rid of someone like that when they still have so much to offer? Charlie Mitten might have been the manager but you got the impression it wasn't just him pulling the strings.'

Mitten, as it turned out, would soon be gone, sacked just a few weeks into the 1961/62 season, but not before he'd created an impression of sorts on Newcastle's relatively new goalkeeper.

'He was clearly a highly talented coach, years before his time really, but he was also a bit of a Jack the Lad as well, a Harry Redknapp type of chap,' recalls Dave. 'He used to have greyhounds running at the Brough Park track in Newcastle. Before one game he offered us the chance to have a bet each. There we were, in his office, in our gear, talking about dogs and which one we were going to back. I was thinking to myself, *Well, this is relaxing*, and I think we might even have gone out and won that particular game. When you look back at these managers and the psychology they employed, maybe that was just Charlie's way of doing things, a bit like the tales you hear of Brian Clough encouraging players to have a beer or a slug of whisky before games.'

In 1961, England's north–south divide was every bit as evident as it is today, socially as much as economically. Realistically, the average Tynesider was about as likely to visit Brighton as they were Brisbane. Other than sections of the M1 and M6, there were no motorways. Car ownership was on the rise but the numbers remained low compared to what would follow later in the decade and during the 1970s. Few had the means to fly internally. Even the railways were starting to feel the pinch as lines began to close, a process that would speed up following publication of the Beeching Report of 1963. People didn't move around as much because they couldn't.

That summer, Dave and Jackie discovered to their pleasant surprise that there was indeed life north of Watford when it came to countryside and coastlines. Beyond the grime of Newcastle there was plenty to see and do relatively close to home in picturesque boltholes such as North Shields, South Shields and the seaside town of Whitley Bay. Further afield, yet easier on the eye still, lay the sand dunes and castle at Bamburgh, the rolling hills of Northumberland, Seahouses with its quaint little harbour and the Holy Island of Lindisfarne. *Why wouldn't anyone want to live up here?* Dave thought to himself on more than a few occasions as the area opened up in front of his eyes.

It's a question that's still being asked well into the 21st century from a football perspective. Since the advent of the Premier League in 1992, the north-east's three largest professional clubs – Middlesbrough, Sunderland and Newcastle United – have all struggled to a greater or lesser extent to attract the very best talent, particularly from abroad (whether that changes with regard to Newcastle's 2021 Saudi-led takeover remains, at the time of writing, to be seen). It was, you may or may not be surprised to learn, ever thus. As far back as the 1950s and 1960s, elite players tended to think twice before committing themselves to the top right-hand corner of England. The very thing that gave the area its unique cultural identity – that feeling of being detached, different, special – was also what worked against it in terms of football recruitment.

'They used to say that if you had any aspiration to play for your country, then you didn't go to Sunderland, Middlesbrough or Newcastle,' says Dave. 'That might not have been the case if you were Scottish because the border was close by, but it certainly applied if you were English or Welsh. The north-east was out of sight, out of mind and you didn't further your progress in football by going there – that was the feeling within the game. We had a couple of Welsh internationals in Ken Leek and Ivor Allchurch but Ken didn't stay long and even Ivor, who was very popular on Tyneside, got to the point where he wanted to go back to Wales. It was just so far away from everywhere else in the days when you could only really get anywhere by train, which is how we used to travel to away games. It didn't bother me in the slightest but it bothered an awful lot of other players.'

The following season, 1961/62, those far-flung journeys by train included such Second Division outposts as Plymouth (a round trip of 820-odd miles), Swansea (approximately 720 miles) and, almost inevitably given this book, Brighton (nearly 700 miles). As disappointing a start as Newcastle suffered to the campaign, slipping as low as 20th in the table towards the end of September, it had nothing on Brighton's wretched decline. On the third Saturday in October, Dave's new paymasters battered his former employer 5-0 at St James' Park. In the return fixture five months later, after Dave had been warmly applauded on to the field by the home supporters, Newcastle piled on the misery once more by winning 4-0, sending Brighton to the foot of the Second Division, where they stayed for the remainder of the season. Having worked so hard to escape the clutches of Third Division South, Brighton returned whence they came to the relatively new Third Division without appearing to put up much of a struggle.

'They always say you should never go back,' reflects Dave. 'I wasn't going back to join Brighton but, on the day of that 4-0 game, I was going back to where it had all started for me as a professional. It was somewhere I cared about deeply, where I'd learned my trade, where I'd met Eric and where I'd played 70-odd games before Newcastle came in for me. Going back for that match, well, it was weird, very weird. Ivor scored a couple but Brighton just didn't seem to offer much resistance. That wasn't the Brighton I remembered.'

Still living in Brighton, Eric Gill had been aware of his local club's increasing plight for almost a year. In May 1961, just weeks after selling Dave to Newcastle and with Brighton having only narrowly avoided relegation, Billy Lane resigned his post as manager, jumping while under pressure rather than waiting to be pushed. In the penultimate week of the 1960/61 season, following a 5-2 defeat to Rotherham, which at the time looked as if it would send Brighton down, Lane had approached Guildford City and enquired about taking Eric back to the Goldstone Ground. It would be one of Lane's last acts as manager and, perhaps unsurprisingly given what had gone before, it would be met with stern resistance from the Southern League club, not to mention incredulity from the player himself.

'It was Albert Tennant, the manager at Guildford, who told me what happened,' remembers Eric. 'We were talking and he said Billy Lane had been in touch wanting me back. He'd offered £2,000 plus another goalkeeper for me. Guildford said, "We don't want your money, or another goalkeeper." He'd clearly let me go too soon, and Dave, and probably a load of other players as well, and he was paying the price on the field in terms of poor results. I wouldn't have gone back anyway. I was doing really well at Guildford. I loved the club, I loved the manager and it suited me fine as I was part-time, on good money, and steadily building my business. He'd run me out of the Football League by not allowing me to sign for anyone else and yet there he was wanting me back. Incredible, just incredible.'

Just how well Eric was doing at Guildford would become clear at the end of the 1961/62 season when City finished a highly creditable third in the Southern League Premier Division, just five points behind first-placed Oxford United (destined to become a Football League club that summer in place of Accrington Stanley, who'd resigned their position in March 1962). Aged just 31, still relatively young for a goalkeeper, Eric was one of Guildford's most consistent performers throughout the campaign – good enough, so Tennant believed, to be playing at a much higher level. 'We're lucky to have him,' City's manager declared. 'There are a number of Football League clubs that would give an arm and a leg to have Eric guarding their goal. Instead the privilege is all ours.'

They say money and morals don't mix. The same principle applies to money and football, yesterday as much as today. In the early 1960s, Brighton & Hove Albion could have reinvested the money they received from healthy attendances, transfers or by releasing players (hence cutting the wage bill) in team strengthening. Yet they chose not to. This might have been down to rank bad management at boardroom level. Or was there something more untoward going on?

'I remember Eric telling me a story about when Albert Mundy went from Brighton to Aldershot and was promised a certain amount of money if he went, money that he didn't end up getting,' says Dave. 'That was how you learned in those days. Forget anything that was said verbally – always get it in writing. That's why we have agents now, to protect players from things like that happening. Let's just say Billy Lane was always motivated by money and I think it was probably his downfall in the end. But he was only human and those were different times. Who knows what pressure he was under from the board as well?'

'In more recent years, I used to go and watch Sussex play cricket down at Hove,' adds Charlie Baker, the man left guarding Brighton's goal following Eric and Dave's departure. 'On one occasion I bumped into Denis Foreman, who used to play cricket for Sussex as well as football for the Albion, and we had quite a chat. I told him I'd just come past Hove station and how it reminded me of matchdays at the football with all the people piling off the trains, heading under the archway and off up to the ground. I said, "They used to be everywhere, thousands and thousands of them." And Denis said, "Yeah, and where did all that money go?" It's a long time ago now, but there were probably questions that needed to be answered.'

Newcastle's disappointing form during the early months of the 1961/62 season meant they were never going to be among the candidates for promotion from a competitive Second Division ultimately won by a Liverpool team enjoying the first fruits of Bill Shankly's managerial wisdom. Nevertheless, in a team struggling to find its feet, Dave certainly excelled, especially once veteran trainer Norman Smith (a fixture at St James' Park since 1938) had replaced Mitten on a temporary basis as manager and injected some fighting spirit into proceedings.

By the time Newcastle travelled to Roker Park on 21 April 1962 for the second Tyne–Wear derby match of the season, any fears of a second successive relegation had long since been banished. They couldn't go up, they couldn't go down – 'only' local pride was at stake. Sunderland, on the other hand, still entertained hopes of promotion and were borderline invincible at home. In short, it had all the makings of a right battle. And so it would prove to be, quite literally in Dave's case.

Five months previously, on the first Saturday of December 1961, Dave had, for the first time since joining Newcastle, gone up against his old nemesis, Brian Clough, who'd switched allegiances by then from Middlesbrough to Sunderland. Different club, same old story in terms of finding the back of the net. That day Clough scored twice in a 2-2 draw, all the while subjecting Dave to his usual bag of intimidatory tricks – the subtle bumps, the odd kick, chasing him around the penalty area, standing in his face whenever the ball was in his hands, you get the picture.

On that occasion, Dave hadn't risen to the bait, but 21 April 1962 would be different.

'About 20 minutes into the game Brian came up to me while I had a live ball in my hands and tried to knock it out of my grasp,' Dave recalls. 'The referee had already gone up to the halfway line, the linesman had turned to run up the line, and there he was trying to do that. I thought, *Well, this isn't on. If he tries that again, I'm going to do something about it.* Ten minutes before half-time up he comes once more, bold as brass. Exactly the same thing happens. The referee turns and runs towards the halfway line, the linesman starts to go as well, there are no TV cameras … so I gave him a right hook between the eyes. He goes flying on to his back. I've still got the ball in my hands, so I go down as though I've been poleaxed as well. The referee isn't sure what's happened. All he knows is the crowd has gone berserk and we're both lying on the ground. So he gives preference to the goalkeeper, blows his whistle and gives us a free kick! At the end, as we were going off, I turned to Brian and said, "We're one-all now."'

In the days that followed, no retrospective action was taken against Dave. The officials hadn't seen the incident. No still photographer had captured it. There was, in short, nothing to review. It didn't matter that thousands of Sunderland supporters in the 57,666 crowd were witnesses. Angry ones at that, despite their team having come away with a 3-0 win. Nobody listens to supporters now. Nobody listened to them then, either.

Sixty years later Dave isn't proud of his actions that day. But he isn't ashamed either. Don't try this at home, kids. On the other hand, never let yourself get pushed around or bullied either.

'I can't say it was an instant reaction because I'd thought about doing something if he tried it again,' Dave confesses. 'In those days goalkeeper was a very physical position to play in, therefore you had to protect yourself. You didn't get any protection from anyone else, least of all referees. It was down to you. As I've said before, back then I was a fairly placid chap off the field but if anyone came into contact with me deliberately on it, then I would react. They were different times and you either stood up for yourself or you got trampled on in every sense of the word.'

'I still can't believe he got away with that,' says Eric, laughing. 'You had to stand up for yourself, absolutely, but even so! He was a bit lucky there.'

Seven days after Dave's Cassius Clay impersonation at Roker Park, Newcastle's season came to an anticlimactic end with a 3-0 home defeat to Leeds United. In hindsight, as has oft been the case at St James' Park over the years, it's perhaps a wonder the team managed to finish as high as 11th in the table given what was happening off the field at the time. Deep in debt, beset by boardroom angst and with angry scenes commonplace outside the club's offices and at shareholder meetings, the Third Division appeared to be a more realistic proposition than any imminent return to the First Division.

With that, so Newcastle United's players sloped away on their summer holidays. All bar one, that is.

8

FROZEN OUT

'We have the power to make this the best
generation of mankind in the history of the
world, or the last' – President John F. Kennedy

IN JUNE 1958, 16 international football teams convened in Sweden to take part in the sixth World Cup finals. Unlike most World Cups, there were no clear favourites. Italy and Spain had failed to qualify. West Germany and Hungary were in the process of rebuilding. No country had ever reached a World Cup Final, let alone won the thing, from outside their own continent, which presumably put Brazil out of the running.

Wrong. Employing a new 4-2-4 formation and fielding a scrawny teenager called Edson Arantes do Nascimento up front, plus a right-winger born with deformities in his legs deemed too irresponsible for his own good by some, Brazil would not only win the trophy but change the way football was perceived forever. By the end of the tournament the world knew Edson simply as Pelé. As for Garrincha, a functioning alcoholic for much of his adult life who'd die before seeing his 50th birthday? 'A phenomenon, capable of sheer magic,' declared one poor unfortunate assigned the task of marking him.

Four years later, when the time came to prepare for the 1962 World Cup finals in Chile, Brazil – so the story goes – contacted the Football Association of Wales with a proposition. In 1958, Wales, more than any other country, had come closest to upstaging the Brazilians, Pelé's 73rd-minute goal separating the two countries in a quarter-final clash that could have gone either way. With Wales having failed to qualify for the 1962 finals and Brazil in need of a European sparring partner to help get them in the groove for Chile, perhaps a friendly or two might be in order?

'You're on,' said Wales, or words to that effect.

So, on Tuesday, 8 May 1962, a full-strength team from the Principality boarded a de Havilland Comet, the world's first commercial jet airliner, at London Airport (Heathrow in today's money) bound for South America. Dave Hollins, called up as reserve to the Welsh number-one goalkeeper Jack Kelsey of Arsenal, had never flown before. Forget about the excitement of setting foot on another continent and the prospect of making your international debut should the top dog come a cropper – just focus on walking up those steps into a jet-propelled metal tube and climbing to 30,000 feet above the Atlantic Ocean.

'It was an amazing experience but quite nerve-racking, let me tell you,' Dave admits. 'In those days nobody went to Majorca or had foreign holidays that involved getting on aeroplanes and flying across Europe or the world. That started to change towards the end of the 1960s but at the start of the decade society was very, very different. Brazil was too far away to make the journey all in one go, so we had to make a stop-off or two on the way. All of a sudden, you're up there looking down on the world. I'm not sure whether anyone had been into space at that point. They certainly hadn't been to the Moon – that was still a long way off. Flying at any kind of height was totally alien as far as the vast majority of people were concerned.'

Wales's team of 1962 consisted of the backbone of the one that had performed so admirably at the 1958 World Cup finals in Sweden. In Kelsey they possessed one of the best goalkeepers in the English top flight. Winger Cliff Jones was an integral part of the Tottenham team that had won the double in 1960/61. Ivor Allchurch may have been plying his trade in the Second Division with Newcastle but remained a force to be reckoned with up front, as did the great John Charles – absent from the 1958 quarter-final due to injury – famously renowned for his defensive capabilities as much as his attacking ones. They might not have qualified for Chile, yet Wales remained among the best of the rest, something the Brazilians fully recognised.

As stunning a coastline as Northumberland boasts, nothing could prepare Dave for the sight and sounds of Rio de Janeiro's Copacabana Beach on the team's first full day in Brazil. Down to the sea they all went, into the sea they all ran, out of the water they all came, only to discover their possessions had vanished.

'Some locals had nicked the lot!' says Dave, laughing. 'And who could blame them, quite frankly. There we were with all the middle- and upper-class people, and you look over towards the end of the beach and there's all the poor people living in shanty towns. We hadn't taken our valuables, so it wasn't as if anything vital had been stolen. Cliff Jones was worried because he'd lost a shirt he really liked but, other than that, it was nothing we couldn't live without.'

The first of two arranged friendlies between Brazil and Wales took place at the Maracanã Stadium, Rio, on 12 May 1962 in front of 100,000 people. Substantially more, you might say, than Dave had been used to while at Brighton, considerably higher even than a typical Tyne–Wear derby attendance of the time. As far as he could see from his substitute's position on the Welsh team bench, there were faces. Brazil, as expected, were dazzling on their way to a 3-1 victory despite being reduced to ten men for most of the second half due to injury, Wales manager Jimmy Murphy rating them a better team than the one that had lifted the trophy in Sweden.

Four days later the two teams met again in São Paulo. Once more Dave was on the bench. Once more Brazil were chillingly brilliant, taking a 35th-minute lead through Vavá. A few minutes later, just after Ivor Allchurch had missed a glorious opportunity to equalise, Jack Kelsey went down at the feet of left-winger Pepe and received a hefty kick in the back for his troubles (some sources suggest the kick came from Vavá, but Dave and others who were there remain adamant it was Pepe). Kelsey continued until half-time before receiving treatment that lasted so long that a linesman had to be dispatched to the dressing room to fetch the Welsh team. When they finally took to the field for the second period, Kelsey was nowhere to be seen.

Opportunity knocks for Dave Hollins.

'Once again, it's a case of going into your own little world,' remembers Dave of his senior international debut. 'The adrenalin starts to flow – it's a lovely word, adrenalin – and you run out on to the pitch in front of this huge crowd. It's an unbelievable feeling, almost like you're running on air. And once you get into the goal, it's all about the ball. Always, always watch the ball. You can't look at the opposition and also watch the ball.'

Even so, at times Dave found he could only marvel at the show being put on in front of him by the Brazilians, especially after Ken Leek had the audacity to equalise in the 62nd minute, momentarily silencing the 80,000 crowd.

'We had "Big John" Charles playing centre-half that day, who was no slouch no matter where he played on the field,' says Dave. 'Most of the time he was marking Pelé and, in the main, doing a pretty good job of it. Then, with about ten minutes to go, Garrincha got hold of the ball out wide and put in this cross. Pelé and "Big John" were standing together somewhere around the penalty spot. And Pelé just rose above him to meet the ball, smacked the thing with his head and sent it whizzing past me like a rocket. It hit the stanchion at the back of the goal before I even knew what had happened. The power he managed to put into it was unbelievable. It was like he jack-knifed in mid-air to get as much force behind the ball as possible.'

Within 60 seconds of the restart Pelé scored again to seal a 3-1 win. Although Brazil deserved their victory, Wales had pushed them hard for long spells, fading only during the closing stages.

On the final whistle, Gilmar, Brazil's outstanding goalkeeper of the period, made a beeline for Dave and gestured with him to swap shirts. 'I'd never heard of the practice before and didn't really know what to do,' Dave confesses. 'The Welsh FA were quite frugal. Giving away items of clothing wasn't the done thing. But Gilmar collected jumpers worn by opposing goalkeepers. So I said, "Yeah, okay," and took mine off and gave it to him, and he gave me his. I came to look on it as quite an honour, especially as it had been my debut, and ended up putting it in a glass frame.'

Rather than stopping at two matches, Wales chose to take the long way home following their exertions in Brazil by accepting an offer to play Mexico, another team preparing for the 1962 World Cup finals, in Mexico City. Three international fixtures across Latin America in the space of ten days (at the end of a long domestic league season), all played in searing heat and, in the case of the latter, at altitude – no wonder many of the Welsh players would far rather have been heading home.

Dave, however, was in his element, especially once he discovered he was going to be sharing a room with John Charles.

'Well, what an honour,' he reflects. 'He was such a big man, an absolute mountain of a chap. And yet, as a player, he was like a ballerina, so light on his feet. When you got off the plane and went through security into whatever country you were visiting, "Big John" was the one they all came to the airport to see. I'll never forget when he took his trousers off – bear with me here – and I said, "Bloody hell, look at your legs!" He said, "This is Italian football for you." His legs were scarred all the way down by the kickings he'd received. But he was a lovely guy and it was a privilege bedding in the same room as him.'

Footballers aren't exactly renowned as singers, as Dave's St James' Park successor Chris Waddle amply demonstrated in 1987 by recording the song 'Diamond Lights' alongside fellow England international Glenn Hoddle. Even in this department, John Charles bucked the trend. Then again, we're talking about someone from Wales here, where singing has long been regarded as a matter of national identity and tradition. If only Waddle had been from Newcastle Emlyn, not Newcastle.

'Wherever we went on that trip, the British embassy in each city would put on a function for all the important so-and-sos,' says Dave. 'I realised later that these were common occurrences for international away games, but of course I was the new boy then. At these dos the players would always be asked to sing the Welsh national anthem and a few of the songs of Wales. That was an experience in itself, listening to these guys. However, I was from Guildford. I didn't know the songs. I realised pretty early on what I needed to do though – stand next to John! He was good at singing. If I stood next to him, then I could just about get away with it.'

Flying for the very first time. Having his clothes stolen on the Copacabana Beach. Facing Pelé. Facing Pepe. Facing Vavá. Facing Garrincha. Experiencing the horror of 'singing' in public when you can't actually sing, even if you have got John Charles there to bail you out. It had been, safe to say, a trip to remember for Dave. There was, however, one more bombshell still to come.

'We were in this huge hotel in Mexico City and, at around four or five in the morning, we all woke up to find it swaying quite violently from side to side,' Dave recalls. 'The door frames were moving, the mirrors, the beds, everything, because we were experiencing an earth tremor. With that, there was panic stations. We were about 15 or 16 storeys up and were down those stairs faster than Olympic sprinters. I remember us standing outside looking up at this hotel as it swayed for what seemed like forever. The buildings out there are built to withstand earthquakes but we were convinced it was going to come tumbling down. And then all of a sudden it stopped.'

That evening, bleary-eyed from the night before and with the temperature at kick-off time nudging 30 degrees, Wales did their level best to match Mexico in what proved to be a feisty encounter before ultimately succumbing 2-1. With Jack Kelsey still injured, Dave took over in goal for the whole match, his first full international start. As it turned out, Kelsey would never play for Wales again. All attempts at rectifying that nasty back injury suffered in São Paulo came to nothing, curbing his career even at club level.

Despite being named as the back-up goalkeeper for the 1962 trip to Brazil and Mexico, Dave was by no means nailed on to take over from Kelsey as Wales's regular No.1. Tony Millington, five years Dave's junior but already a regular at West Bromwich Albion, lurked in the wings. Ultimately, the two men would learn to share the position over the next 18 months, with something of a friendly three-way jostle for the jersey developing once the even younger Gary Sprake began to establish himself at Leeds United.

'As a goalkeeper, Jack had been one of the best,' says Cliff Jones, one of the last surviving members of the Wales teams from that era. 'Before he took up football full-time, he'd worked in the steelworks in Swansea as a smelter. His hands were huge, like irons, and of course that's a big help if you're going to play in goal. But I have to say he was one of the worst kickers of a football you could ever wish to see! After we had our training sessions, we used to have five-a-side kick-arounds and nobody wanted Jack on their side because he was so useless. Handling the ball – yes. Kicking the ball – no. That's something Dave brought to us which Jack couldn't – an ability to kick. Dave was a smashing character who didn't fall into that "all goalkeepers are crazy" bracket. He was intelligent, outgoing, very friendly and chatty. And of course he came from a footballing family. We felt quite safe with him around. We felt we were in good hands.'

* * *

There's a well-known song by Billy Joel, the American singer and pianist, called 'We Didn't Start the Fire', which lists 118 key cultural, political, scientific, social and sporting events spanning 1949 (the year of Joel's birth) and 1989 when the track was recorded. At the seat of Joel's fire sits 1962. It was, after all, a year that 'crystallised the growing tension between the old and new', to quote writer and historian Juliet Nicolson, when the very real prospect of nuclear conflict threatened to turn our planet into a wasteland. In the event of there being no positive solution to the Cuban Missile Crisis, games masters on the playing fields of British schools were asked to tell pupils to kneel and turn away from the direction of any blast cloud. As if that was going to make a shred of difference in the long run. Small wonder large numbers of young people took to wearing flowers in their hair as the decade wore on in solidarity with the peace and counterculture movements.

But we, I, digress …

Absent from Billy's list was the great British freeze of late 1962 and early 1963. Hardly surprising, really, given the piano man grew up in Long Island and would have been 13 at the time. That's not to say, however, that the freeze was any less significant than many of Billy's other references.

As night fell on Boxing Day 1962, so snow began to fall across parts of southern England, spreading to all corners of the UK over the following days. It kept snowing for the next ten weeks. Everything, needless to say, ground to a halt. Animals perished. People perished. Schools closed. Rivers froze. Even the sea around parts of the coastline iced over. Between 23 December and 1 March, Newcastle United played one solitary match (in relatively temperate Plymouth). Yet, with people's lives and livelihoods on the line, sport didn't really matter one iota. Football's place in the grand scheme of things became, quite literally, crystal clear.

'We had some severe winters while we were living up in Newcastle, especially compared to what we were used to in the south of England, but that was the only one where we struggled to get out of the front door,' remembers Dave. 'There was four or five feet of snow piled high against it. It was incredible. We didn't train much because we couldn't, maybe a few times out on the coast on the sands. We didn't

even have any central heating in our house! My job in the
winters before I went training would always be to light the
three coal fires to keep things warm. The coal man we
used was absolutely brilliant but that particular winter he
really earned his money. He'd haul the coal through the
garage into the coal bunker and it was the best coal you
could ever think of. It burned really well. Then we'd give
him a cup of tea or coffee as a thank you.'

'And I couldn't understand a word he said in all
the years we were there,' admits Jackie. 'I came to
understand most Geordie accents, which can be really
strong, but not that one. All you could do was nod along
and smile whenever he spoke. He must have thought we
were mad!'

At the opposite end of England, it's said that an
enterprising local builder with connections to Brighton &
Hove Albion attempted to defrost the Goldstone Ground
pitch using his own personal tarmac-laying equipment.
The pitch, or at least the grass, supposedly failed to
withstand the experiment. Nevertheless, Brighton did
somehow manage to stage three home matches during
January and February 1963, generally faring better
throughout the freeze than Guildford City based just 45
miles to the north-west.

On the plus side, no football meant Eric had more
time for his guests – except that he didn't have any. With
temperatures outside so low that people daren't leave their
homes, only the insane – or perhaps an Eskimo – would
have considered a few days away on the Sussex coast.
Which is a shame, as Eric and Ida now had more space
than ever before.

'All the money I got from playing football I put back into the business,' says Eric. 'After a while we got the chance to move up a bit in the world. I sold The Perrimay and bought a small hotel on Marine Parade – Simpson's, it was called. A few years later I bought the one next door and knocked them together. So now we had a 40-room hotel right smack bang on Brighton seafront with all the rooms overlooking the sea. That did all your advertising for you. It's still there, only now it's called Drakes. We had car parking as well. If you know Brighton, then you'll know parking a car there can be murder. More and more people were starting to own cars, so that became a real asset. People would drive along, see our hotel, see that we had parking and go, "Cor, we'll pull in there."

'But it was hard work, twice as much work as being a goalkeeper. Being part-time at Guildford meant I was more hands-on and it never stopped, 24 hours a day, seven days a week. The times I had to get out of bed in the middle of the night when the bell rang because somebody wanted something. But I ran it as best I could with Ida, and the kids started helping out as well as they got older. We rarely had any trouble though. As long as you give the customer what they want, especially when it comes to food, they'll be happy.'

'Eric won't like me reminding him of this but there was one time when some guy came down from London with his family and parked his car right across the drive where Eric's guests used to park their cars,' recalls Dave. 'Eric had told him, "Look, this is my hotel, you can't park your car willy-nilly here all day." And this guy hit him, sprawled him out. These things can, and sometimes do, happen. But that, as far as I'm aware, was a one-off. Eric and Ida ran a happy ship but it can't have been easy for either of them, especially while Eric was playing football, even part-time. The demands must have been huge. But he made a success of it, he really did. And he deserved that success.'

The respect ran both ways. 'You could see he was starting to have a really good career but that didn't surprise me in the slightest,' says Eric, reflecting on Dave's progress at international as well as club level. 'He was a natural. It just came to him. Some are manufactured players and some are natural players. If you've got natural skill, then it's almost like you don't have to try. Dave was a natural. He was made to be a goalkeeper.'

In June 1962, four months prior to the Cuban Missile Crisis and six before the big freeze set in, Dave had arrived back on Tyneside from his Latin American adventures to discover a new manager in charge of Newcastle United. Norman Smith's somewhat extended 'temporary' stint at the helm was over. In his seat sat a man whose contribution to the Newcastle United cause remains right up there alongside that of Jackie Milburn, Kevin Keegan, Alan Shearer et al. His name was Joe Harvey.

Born in the Yorkshire mining village of Edlington, Harvey was Newcastle's captain and defensive cornerstone throughout the mid-to-late 1940s and the club's halcyon days of the early 1950s. A tough, rugged character who abhorred losing, he was, in the words of the club's long-standing official historian Paul Joannou, someone that 'always pushed to the limit and made sure his colleagues did the same'. Direct, honest, great sense of humour, a smoker, no stranger to a pre-match pint of Guinness on a Saturday lunchtime – that was Joe.

Having cut his managerial teeth at cash-strapped Barrow and Workington, Harvey first applied for the Newcastle position in 1958 only to lose out to Charlie Mitten. On the verge of quitting the game and focusing instead on his newsagent business in Newcastle, he nevertheless chose to throw his hat in the ring when the job was advertised again in May 1962. This time he was successful, taking up the position (initially on a 12-month trial) on the first day of June.

While the world argued and, in the case of Britain, froze, so Harvey set about the slightly more parochial task of rebuilding Newcastle United's team in his mould. Out went many old familiar faces, Ivor Allchurch among them, and in came the likes of forward Dave Hilley and midfielder Jim Iley, who between them would clock up in excess of 450 appearances for the club over the seasons to come. Before October was out, Harvey's evolving team had amply demonstrated what they were capable of, administering tennis-like 6-1, 6-0 and 6-0 thrashings to Middlesbrough, Walsall and Swansea Town, respectively. Defensively, the odd hiccup remained, four goals being conceded on three separate occasions prior to Christmas, but by and large Newcastle and their Surrey/Welsh goalkeeper reached the season's mid-point in rude health and with every chance of gaining promotion.

At which point the snows came. When the thaw finally arrived in March, so too did the matches – and then some. Even with the season being extended to account for the colossal backlog of fixtures, clubs still found themselves with two, three or occasionally four matches to play per week.

Initially Newcastle managed to ride the wave, marking their return to action with a hard-fought goalless draw at Sunderland in which Dave saved a first-half penalty in front of 62,420 paying punters – white-hot atmosphere, stupidly cold-air temperature. However, three defeats from four matches in the space of 11 days during the second half of April ultimately scuppered any hopes they had of catching the leading pack. All told, a seventh-place finish in the Second Division still represented an improvement on the mid-table obscurity of the previous season.

Two years after arriving at St James' Park and just a couple of games short of 100 appearances for the club, Dave's consistency and good form since arriving from Brighton had so far exempted him from the wholesale changes taking place within Newcastle's dressing room. But that didn't necessarily mean he felt at ease. At the time it was reported in the local press that Dave was at loggerheads with the club over wages, something he flatly denies today. What he did find unsettling were the managerial changes and the effect they were ultimately likely to have on his future.

'Every time a new manager comes into a club, they always like to stamp their authority on the team by bringing in their own players,' says Dave. 'That's the case as much today as it was then. In less than two years I'd gone through Charlie Mitten, Norman Smith and now I was on to Joe Harvey. In that time just about all the players who'd been there when I first arrived had gone. Naturally that's going to make you think, *Well, where does that leave me?* When you go through three managers, you can bet there's going to be one of them who doesn't fancy you. I got the feeling Joe Harvey was that one.'

In the summer of 1963 Dave's hunch came to pass when Harvey went out and bought Gordon Marshall, a goalkeeper born in the English Home Counties but who'd established himself as arguably the best stopper in Scotland with Heart of Midlothian.

'I think I reminded Joe too much of my predecessor, Ronnie Simpson, who Joe had known from his own playing days at Newcastle,' Dave suggests. 'Ronnie was a very spectacular, acrobatic type of goalkeeper, and I was the same. I think Joe probably analysed me, the goalkeeper he'd inherited, and thought, *We got rid of one chap like that and brought in another one. Why do that?* Gordon was a big lad who commanded his box well, but he wasn't very athletic. As a goalkeeper, you're rarely both. But Joe wanted a change of approach and Gordon's style suited that approach.'

Something else that worked against Dave during his time at Newcastle, very much in common with Eric's twilight with Brighton & Hove Albion, was the cumulative effect of some pretty serious injuries on his body, a reminder of how risky goalkeeping could be, even with referees starting to afford them greater degrees of protection.

'We played one match down in Plymouth when I went to my near post to deal with a corner kick,' says Dave. 'Some chap came up right behind me and smashed me into the post. Of course, my shoulder just shot straight out. I was sidelined for a good three or four months with that. Worse still was when I dived at someone's feet in a match at Sheffield United – at least I'm pretty certain it was Sheffield United. Unfortunately, the other fellow followed through and cracked three or four of my ribs. The one thing I do remember for certain is that I ended up in hospital in Rotherham. We got on the team coach and I was in agony. I said to Joe Harvey, "I'm going to have to go to hospital." So they dropped me off at Rotherham and I was in there for about a week. I've still got a rib that sticks out at a funny angle from that. You always remember the big hits but there were plenty of other knocks to my legs, knees and what have you. I ended up being pretty unlucky with injuries.'

'That was the only time I remember being really worried about him,' adds Jackie Hollins. 'I was expecting him home and, of course, he didn't turn up. Someone came round and said, "We've left him down there because he's broken his ribs." But it didn't put me off going to watch him. When he was at the Albion, all the wives used to sit in the stand together. It never crossed my mind that he might get seriously injured. His dad, who was a wonderful man, had always told him, "Son, if it's a 50-50 ball, let 'em have it!" That's the way Dave used to play. I never really stopped to think he could be the one who'd come off worse.'

Unlike a fair percentage of planet Earth's population, Dave has no idea where exactly he was when news of President John F. Kennedy's assassination in Dallas began filtering through late on Friday, 22 November 1963. Then again, this supposedly unforgettable moment in history did coincide almost exactly with Joe Harvey shunting him off into the reserves at St James' Park, so it's not as if our man didn't have other things on his mind.

Dave would play only ten league and cup matches that season. The following campaign, 1964/65, Newcastle United regained their place in the top flight of English football by winning the Second Division, with Gordon Marshall ever-present in the team. Dave, in other words, didn't get to make a single appearance. Not one. Talk about feeling like an uninvited guest at your own party.

Professional footballers, by and large, tend to go one of two ways on being ousted from their natural environment by another player. Way number one – and this applies as much in the 21st century as it did in 1963, by which time the rights of footballers were slowly improving – involves the good old-fashioned sulk. The sulk comes on different levels. There's walking around the place wearing a long face through to the more nuclear variations, for instance actively stirring up bad feeling among team-mates in the dressing room. Regardless of strata, the sulk nearly always ends in a hastily arranged transfer.

Way number two, however, is to make the best of a bad situation. Again, this comes on different levels. Some players choose to knuckle down and fight to regain their place in the team. Others choose to knuckle down, fight to regain their place in a team AND go the extra mile in other areas, either to curry favour with the boss or simply because it's in their DNA.

Before the ink was even dry on Gordon Marshall's contract, Dave had opted for way number two ... with knobs on. He chose to knuckle down, fight to regain his place in the team and go the extra mile around St James'

Park, not necessarily to stay in Joe Harvey's good books but because he was, and always will be, a nice guy. If a striker wanted some extra shooting practice after training, Dave would volunteer to work with him. The same applied to defenders or anyone else looking to put in an extra shift requiring a goalkeeper.

Newcastle's youngsters, fresh from winning the FA Youth Cup in 1962, felt the benefit of Dave's presence perhaps more than most, thanks to his willingness to stay behind at the club's (now former) training ground in Benwell long after the other senior professionals had left for home, or the bookies, or the races. From the autumn of 1963 to the summer of 1965, Dave's selfless professionalism had zero effect on Joe Harvey's team selections but it did make him one of the most popular players on Newcastle United's payroll.

'When I first joined Newcastle, I went into the reserve team, which is what David was in after Gordon Marshall had arrived,' recalls Frank Clark, who, prior to winning almost everything there is to win at club level with Nottingham Forest under Brian Clough, made 457 appearances for Newcastle. 'I was 19, not long out of school and a bit of a greenhorn. And Dave befriended me. He kind of looked after me, which is something I needed as it was a bit of a culture shock, as you can imagine. He didn't have to do that, but he did. He was very helpful. I know I'm not the only one from that time who owes him a debt of gratitude.'

Cast into the wilderness at Newcastle, at least Dave had his very own parallel universe to fall back on in the shape of the Welsh national team. Today, it's relatively common in football's upper echelons for clubs to have three, four or sometimes more goalkeepers of varying nationalities on their books. Squad rotation means even regular first-choice keepers occasionally find themselves being 'rested', in management speak. It's not unusual, in other words, to come upon international goalkeepers who aren't playing regular first-team football for their clubs. In the early to mid-1960s, it was virtually unheard of.

With Dave playing reserve-team football at St James' Park it would have been so, so easy for Wales manager Jimmy Murphy (who juggled his international post alongside that of assistant to Matt Busby at Manchester United) to cast him adrift and lean instead on his two other options, Tony Millington and Gary Sprake. That Murphy chose instead to rotate the three goalkeepers was testimony to Dave's performances at Newcastle prior to being replaced by Gordon Marshall and indeed for Wales since his international baptism in Latin America. Twice he'd been called upon during the early months of 1963 to face, first, Hungary in a European Nations' Cup qualifier (the forerunner to the modern-day European Championship, or Euros) and, second, Northern Ireland in the Home International Championship (the annual competition between England, Scotland, Wales and Ireland – or latterly Northern Ireland – which ceased in 1984). On both occasions Dave had performed well, with Wales holding the Magyars to a 1-1 draw in Cardiff before thrashing Northern Ireland 4-1 in Belfast.

England at Ninian Park, Cardiff, on 12 October 1963, with the Cuban Missile Crisis ramping up ominously as a backdrop, proved to be a slightly tougher proposition.

'Gordon Banks, Jimmy Armfield, Ray Wilson, Jimmy Greaves, Bobby Smith, Bobby Moore, Bobby Charlton ... yeah, the foundations of a pretty good team there,' says Dave, laughing. Which is certainly more than he did that day. The match reports tell of the many fine saves Dave produced during the second half. Unfortunately, they also detail how he lost his footing in the fifth minute just as Greaves was teeing up the cross that enabled Smith to head England into a 1-0 lead.

'That slip of his early on set Wales on the road to defeat, for goalkeepers above all can't redeem themselves,' wrote Dewi Lewis in the *Western Mail* prior to detailing how the Welsh fell apart during the final 25 minutes to lose 4-0. For what it's worth, the third goal, scored by Bobby Charlton, sent the Manchester United midfielder above Nat Lofthouse and Tom Finney to the top of England's all-time scoring charts, putting him on 31. If you're going to lose heavily, then at least make sure one of the goals you concede is destined for the history books, scored by a great man.

'He was in another league that day,' is how Dave describes Charlton's glittering performance against a Welsh team without the injured John Charles, still a hugely influential figure despite his 31 years and the degenerative effects of being one of the most fouled players in world football. 'But the other thing which really stands out in my memory happened right at the end. Remember how Gilmar had come up to me after my debut in Brazil and asked to swap shirts? Well, Gordon Banks did exactly the same thing. As I said, I hadn't known this was something goalkeepers did, but it turned out he collected them too.

When someone like Gordon Banks walks up and says, "Dave, do you mind if I have your shirt?" you're not exactly going to say no, are you?'

When Dave Bowen, who as a player had captained Wales to the last eight of the 1958 World Cup finals, took over from Murphy as manager of the Welsh international team in 1964, he too chose to rotate the three goalkeepers despite Dave continuing to play second fiddle to Gordon Marshall at Newcastle. If ever one or more of them was unavailable (fairly often in the case of Gary Sprake through his league and cup commitments at upwardly mobile Leeds United), then there was always someone else in the fold who could take over. And, if that goalkeeper played particularly well for Wales, then they would usually be given first dibs on the shirt next time around. In terms of creating a stable defensive environment, it shouldn't have worked. Yet somehow it did. What's more, the arrangement appeared to suit all three players, Dave in particular, starved as he was of first-team football at Newcastle.

'They each had their particular strengths and weaknesses but they were all good goalkeepers,' says Cliff Jones. 'I may be wrong but Tony didn't figure quite as much as Dave or Gary. Gary was a tremendous goalkeeper and a smashing character but you wouldn't mess with him. He could certainly look after himself. I even remember him confronting a supporter once over something. But after Jack Kelsey had retired and until Gary came through, or whenever he was unavailable, it was Dave who usually kept goal for us. And he rarely let us down.'

'We were all different, and I don't just mean as goalkeepers,' adds Dave. 'Gary was someone who could certainly look after himself, a good goalkeeper though who would go on to establish himself in a very successful Leeds side. As for Tony, he had a terrible habit of smoking. People smoked then, more so than they do today, but even allowing for that Tony was horrendous. He smoked like a chimney! I think it must have been something to do with his nervous system – goalkeeping can do that to you. Whatever it was, there always seemed to be a cigarette in his hand.

'But I have to say, I had the time of my life being part of the Wales set-up. We all respected each other – not just us goalkeepers, but all the players. There were none of the internal rivalries which you sometimes find with international sides. You know, little cliques of players from particular clubs or places who only speak to each other. We were one, more like a club side really. I kept in touch with quite a few of the players. After Ivor [Allchurch] died a few years ago, Jackie and I went down to Swansea and spent time with his wife, Esme, who was such a wonderful woman. Oh, it was brilliant, playing for Wales, such a privilege. They're still some of my most cherished memories.'

9

1966 AND ALL THAT

'If you don't like us, don't accept our invitations
and don't invite us to come to see you. Whether
you like it or not, history is on our side. We will
bury you.' – Nikita Khrushchev

CAST YOUR mind back to Chapter 3, if you will.
Remember that bit about how, in terms of sheer mountains
to climb, you had to go some to beat the annual scramble
for promotion from the lower echelons of the Football
League? Well, that mountain may well have had an equally
daunting twin peak concealed in the mists of England's
non-league football scene.

Up until 1986, the worst-placed clubs in the Football
League had to go through an annual process known as
re-election, which worked something like this. Imagine
for a few moments that you are chair of Hopeless United,
a cash-strapped club in English football's fourth tier. It's
1964. Not for the first time, Hopeless have finished the
season in the bottom four places and must now reapply for
their place in the Football League. In a couple of weeks'

time, league members will vote at their annual general meeting on whether Hopeless should remain in the fourth tier or be replaced by one of several ambitious non-league clubs applying to join the Football League. Your job at that meeting is to sweet-talk as many other chairmen as possible (and they would all have been men in 1964) into voting for Hopeless United. Failure to suck up in the appropriate manner (i.e. plying those chairmen and their directors with the finest champagne and/or whisky available to humanity) could well put the club's future in jeopardy.

In reality, re-election worked very much along the same lines as that old idiom about turkeys voting for Christmas. Hartlepool United were once so bad they went cap in hand to their Football League peers 11 times in the space of 28 years. On each occasion, they were successfully re-elected. Between 1958 (when the Third Division South and Third Division North became the Third and Fourth Divisions) and 1986 (when automatic promotion and relegation to and from the Football League was introduced), five clubs failed in their bids to be re-elected. The risk was there, in other words. But it was minimal. When you stop to consider the small army of non-league clubs that applied unsuccessfully in that time to be elected, five is a pretty sorry figure.

One of the unfortunate handful happened to be Newcastle United's near neighbours Gateshead, who in 1960 failed in their bid to be re-elected and were replaced by Peterborough United.

Guess how many times Peterborough United had to apply to become a member of the Football League before they were finally admitted?

Twenty-one.

That's an awful lot of angst and frustration and rejection and wasted time before other people finally come around to your way of thinking.

Between 1960 and 1968, Guildford City applied on seven separate occasions to be elected to the Football League. Seven times their application was rejected. They received a few votes here and there but never enough to seriously trouble the clubs finishing 89th, 90th, 91st and 92nd in the Football League.

If it was ever going to happen, then 1965 was probably the year. Having finished second in the Southern League Premier Division behind champions Weymouth, Guildford went to work on their election bid hoping the presence of several ex-Football League players in their team, including Eric Gill, might just tip things in their favour. Nothing like having a few friends in high places. Weymouth, conveniently, had already decided not to seek election. The stars, so it seemed, were aligning behind Guildford's cause.

Alas, astrologers occasionally make mistakes. At the Football League's annual general meeting, Lincoln City, Stockport County, Barrow and Halifax Town – the clubs occupying the Fourth Division's bottom four places – polled 48, 45, 41 and 41 votes, respectively. Guildford City received just three. Even Bedford Town, who sought election despite finishing 11 points and eight places below Guildford in the Southern League Premier Division table, received four votes. When it came to rewarding mediocrity bordering on downright failure, the re-election process really took the biscuit.

'The Football League was a closed shop,' says Eric. 'The clubs that were in there didn't want anyone else joining. They were happy to let the bottom teams stay, no matter how poorly they were doing. We [Guildford City] always seemed to be doing well towards the top of the Southern League but it never happened. I remember Oxford United going up one year but they were more the exception to the rule – they were only admitted because Accrington Stanley had gone bust. It didn't bother me so much because I was really happy being part-time, getting good money and concentrating on my business. It was the perfect situation for me. But it was a shame for the other players and the people behind the club who I know were putting in their own money. It would have been nice to see their efforts rewarded. But it was never going to happen.'

Guildford City's final placings in the Premier Division of the Southern League spanning the seasons 1960/61 to 1965/66, Eric's final campaign as the club's regular first-choice goalkeeper, were 15th, 3rd, 4th, 2nd and 16th. In 1968/69, venting money, not to mention morale, having plugged away for so long with such little reward (they also finished 6th and 5th in 1966/67 and 1967/68, respectively), City washed up last and were relegated for the first time in the club's history. The 'golden period', as it later became known among supporters, was over.

'We got pretty good attendances at the time, especially for a non-league club, but as well as we did on the field the club couldn't survive on the money coming in through the turnstiles alone,' reflects Eric. 'That was never going to be enough. I'd imagine most non-league clubs at that time survived through the generosity of one or two people, and Guildford were no exception in that department. We had directors who put in money out of their own pockets. They were very good, very generous. But that can only go on for so long. Nobody's pockets are bottomless, are they?'

'When I was growing up my dream was to play football at Joseph's Road, home of Guildford City, my local team,' says Dave Hollins. 'I remember going down there as a child many times. On one occasion a group of pretty raucous lads turned up. One of them clearly drew the short straw and, just before half-time, jumped over the barrier and threw a bucket of water over Merthyr's trainer, a long-haired guy who always had this big bucket and a sponge with him. This fella tore off after the lad, chasing him all round the track, which went around the pitch and out of the ground! Great memories. They had some illustrious players there over the years, including Eric. It would have been wonderful if they'd been accepted into the Football League when he was there, but it wasn't to be. Re-election and the way it worked made that more or less impossible.'

As a boy he'd dreamed of playing in the quaint if parochial surroundings of Joseph's Road. Come 1965, Dave was getting his hands dirty inside some much larger and more celebrated arenas, albeit for Wales rather than Newcastle United where Gordon Marshall continued, at least for now, to hold sway. In mid-March Dave was back between the posts at Ninian Park in Cardiff for a vital World Cup qualifier against Greece, a match the Welsh won 4-1 to keep alive their hopes of making the finals in England the following year. Two weeks later he was outstanding at Windsor Park, Belfast, in the 5-0 demolition of Northern Ireland in the Home International

Championship, making several important early saves while the scoreline was goalless.

The only cloud, a small one at that, had been Tony Millington getting the nod to play against England at Wembley the previous November. 'That would have been nice but I was substitute that night,' recalls Dave. 'So I made it to Wembley but I didn't get to play. You can't win them all!'

The decision over where to stage the World Cup finals of 1966 had been made in Rome back in August 1960, with England edging rival bids from Spain and West Germany. England, being hosts, qualified automatically. For the other home nations the mere fact it was being held next door – the first World Cup ever to take place in an English-speaking country – provided every incentive to be there. Like Cinderella, everyone wanted to go to the ball.

Drawn in a qualification group alongside the USSR, Greece and Denmark, Wales nevertheless seemed to go out of their way to make life difficult for themselves from the word go. In October 1964, missing several key players and with Millington in goal, they'd been guilty of complacency as much as lethargy against Denmark's part-timers in Copenhagen, losing 1-0. The following month, with Gary Sprake between the posts, Greece went and beat them 2-0 in Athens, a result that left Wales not so much needing to get out of jail but to escape from Alcatraz to make the finals.

By the time Greece came to Cardiff for the return fixture on 17 March 1965, it was Dave's turn to keep goal. That 4-1 win, combined with the 5-0 triumph in Belfast a fortnight later, put him in the driver's seat for the match against the USSR in Moscow on 30 May. Anything less than a win or a draw against the group favourites and Wales would, effectively, be kissing the 1966 World Cup finals goodbye.

At the beginning of May, an under-strength Wales travelled to Florence to face Italy in a warm-up match ahead of the impending qualifier later that month. Having managed to hold the Italians in sweltering conditions for most of the match, the Welsh wilted badly during the latter stages to lose 4-1. Dave was about the only Wales player to get anything out of the exercise, pulling off several impressive saves in the Tuscan sun. Strange as it might sound, goalkeepers sometimes feel better about themselves after a backs-to-the-wall encounter in which they've conceded goals than they do having kept a clean sheet and had zilch to do. Florence was just such an occasion for Dave.

… and so to Moscow.

'Moscow, I have to say, was a pretty horrible place to be at that time,' says Dave. 'Don't forget this was only 20 years after the end of the Second World War, right at the height of the Cold War. Nobody had anything because there was no money to spend. There was no traffic on the streets as nobody had any cars. It was so bleak, like something out of a spy novel. Architecturally, though, the place was fantastic. I'd been away a few times by then with Wales, and I've been abroad a few times since on my holidays, but I've never seen anything architecturally like that, what with all those ornate designs and gothic-style buildings. You couldn't help but think, *If these walls could talk*, as there's so much history surrounding you.'

Being international football players, the Welsh were received in Moscow as official guests of the Soviet Union and its ruling Communist Party. This, as you might imagine, proved to be something of a double-edged sword. On the one hand, it gave them a pass into certain corners of Russian culture and society that they might not otherwise have experienced. On the other, not everything they saw was necessarily to their taste.

'We were taken to the circus and the ballet,' remembers Dave. 'The ballet in particular – and we're talking about the Bolshoi Ballet here – had a real effect on me. I'd never been to anything like that before in my life. It was simply beautiful and very majestic. All that balance, stamina, poise, so much discipline in every movement they made. It was like watching finely tuned athletes, which, I suppose, is what they were. I will never forget that for as long as I live. But then you also had Lenin.'

Lenin?

'Yes, Lenin. He'd been lying in state for years by then. One day we were told that we were going to see him. Apparently, Muscovites were encouraged to go and see the body once every year – that, according to our guide, was the rule. And now it was our turn. Being visiting dignitaries, we jumped the queue, which was bad enough. You had all these poor people living in what seemed to be quite difficult conditions queueing up and we were led straight past them. As you'd expect, it was very solemn. We were standing there, right beside the body, watching the local people traipse past, bowing their heads, some of them weeping. It made me feel very uncomfortable and I know I wasn't alone. He's still lying there now, except the surroundings have been somewhat modernised. Apparently, it's totally different and less austere. It was very alien to us, the whole scenario. I honestly found it quite horrendous.'

The evening before the match, having completed a full training session at the Lenin Stadium prior to attending the Bolshoi Ballet, Dave and his team-mates were taken to the kind of restaurant most Muscovites could only dream of stepping inside. After dinner the team returned to their hotel and went to bed. Well, most of them did. Dave, however, spent the majority of the night in his bathroom, on the toilet, with diarrhoea. Come sunrise, he was in absolutely no fit state to play a game of football.

Now, diarrhoea, it should be said, can strike at any time, any place. This, though, was the USSR in 1965, in the context of a must-win football match for both countries, at a point in history when all manner of espionage and one-upmanship was going on between east and west. Is it at all possible that some kind of jiggery-pokery involving restaurant food might have taken place the night before the match? Dave reckons not, although he can't be 100 per cent sure.

'I don't think so. There was so much squalor there at that time. You couldn't believe how bad things were. You had queues just to get bread. I reckon it was a one-off and I simply ate something that was infected. By that, I mean food that had gone bad, rather than infected with something suspicious. I didn't stop to think whether it might have been anything else. I certainly hope it wasn't anything else! I suppose you can never be absolutely sure when it comes to Russia, as we've seen in much more recent times. It's quite incredible what kind of people they are – not the average man in the street – but the regime they have there. They're quite capable of anything.'

That evening Wales took to the pitch inside the Lenin Stadium with Tony Millington wearing the No.1 shirt, having at least had the foresight to bring a substitute goalkeeper. In torrential rain and before 100,000 spectators – none of them Welsh – the USSR took a first-half lead and then doubled their advantage three minutes after the break when Graham Williams of West Bromwich Albion put through his own net. Although Bolton Wanderers striker Wyn Davies subsequently reduced the deficit, Wales were unable to find the equaliser they so desperately needed to keep their World Cup qualification hopes alive.

Five months later, with Gary Sprake in goal, Wales managed to exact some revenge over the USSR by winning 2-1 in Cardiff. Five weeks after that, with Dave back in the team, they saw off a spirited yet defensively naïve Danish team 4-2 in Wrexham. But the damage had already been done. The USSR progressed to the World Cup finals in England with Wales finishing second, the concept of play-offs for group runners-up still light years away. The dream of playing in a World Cup on familiar soil was over.

'It was a disappointment, but not that disappointing,' Dave confides. 'You see, the attitude among players was totally different in those days. Today, when you go to a match or watch it on TV, everything is so hyped up. Everything is so dramatic. When a team loses, it's treated almost like there's been a death in the family. In those days that sort of attitude didn't exist. You played for your club or your country, and if the result was there, it was there. If it wasn't, then it wasn't. You did your best but when you walked off the field and went home, there it ended. That probably sounds strange in the context of today but it's just the way it was. We had some illustrious players in the Wales team, some amazing talent, but we didn't qualify. Russia did – end of. It really was as clear-cut as that.'

And so Dave kept himself busy during the summer of 1966 watching the World Cup finals on his black-and-white television at home in Newcastle, following the fortunes of a group of players – many of whom he knew well – as they chased World Cup glory. Of course, he wanted England to win the thing, despite keeping goal for Wales. Football, as we touched on in Chapter 5 with the Munich air disaster, really was far less tribal then than it is today. Anyhow, Dave had lived his entire life on the eastern side of Offa's Dyke, the 177-mile-long earthwork that roughly divides England from Wales. To not want England to win, especially with Wales out of the equation, would have just been plain weird.

Having said that, England's third goal in the 4-2 win over West Germany in the final, Geoff Hurst's second of the match, the one that came down off the underside of the crossbar over the line in extra time ...

'It really wasn't over the line, never in a million years,' Dave maintains.

... but then you might expect a goalkeeper, someone whose duty it is to prevent goals, to say that.

'Geoff wasn't a great player but he was there at that time and he took his chance,' adds Dave. 'A situation arose where he got to step into the team in place of Jimmy Greaves, and he went with it. Jimmy was one of the greatest goalscoring machines ever, as I knew to my cost. But Geoff came into the team in the latter stages of the tournament in place of him and scored two or three goals in the final, depending on whether you think it crossed the line. I don't think it did and the technology we have now would probably confirm that, although it would probably take four or five minutes of looking at it on various screens to decide. And that's wrong as well – football's supposed to be a game of momentum. England won the cup though, so everyone was happy, me included.'

* * *

The season prior to England winning the World Cup, 1965/66, had marked Newcastle United's return to domestic football's penthouse after a four-year absence. Back in the high life again, Joe Harvey's team won three, drew two and lost four of their opening nine league matches, all with Gordon Marshall in goal.

Twenty-two months had now passed since Dave had last started a first-team match for the Magpies. That's a long time to spend in the shadows away from the roar of your club's supporters, even if you're getting the occasional atmospheric fix on the international scene.

President Kennedy's assassination. 'Beatlemania'. Cassius Clay becoming Muhammad Ali. Richard Burton marrying Elizabeth Taylor (for the first time). The escalation of the war in Vietnam. Nelson Mandela being sentenced to life imprisonment. The Great Train Robbery. Martin Luther King Jr becoming the youngest recipient of the Nobel Peace Prize. The death of Winston Churchill. Bob Dylan outraging folk purists by going electric. A Labour government coming to power in Britain for the first time in 13 years. The Watts Riots. Sidney Poitier becoming the first African-American male to win an Academy Award. The disappearance of five children in and around Manchester in a case known as the Moors Murders. Radio Caroline beginning regular broadcasts from the North Sea. All of this and much, much more had played out on the world's stage since Dave's name last appeared on a Newcastle United first XI team sheet.

In the week leading up to their away match against Chelsea on Saturday, 25 September 1965, Newcastle had conspired to lose 4-3 at home to Third Division Peterborough United in the League Cup, a result that brought about changes in the team for the trip to west London. Marshall wasn't officially among those dropped, suffering as he was from a reported heavy cold, but the infection made it easier for Joe Harvey to recall his Welsh international back-up goalkeeper from the wilderness. Not only that, but Newcastle's manager also made him captain for the afternoon in a decision that appears to have been made from the heart rather than any tactical reasoning, Dave's younger brother John having graduated through Chelsea's ranks to become club captain at the age of just 19.

So it came to pass that Dave and John walked side by side on to the pitch at Stamford Bridge in front of their respective teams, trying to maintain an air of straight-faced professionalism when all they wanted to do was smile at where destiny had taken them. Invited to shake hands by referee David Smith (who also told Dave to change out of his all-black jersey into a more conventional green top before kick-off), there the conviviality ended and 'the battle of Stamford Bridge', as one newspaper described it, began. According to the correspondent from *The Times*:

> What took place in the intervening 90 minutes was only distantly related to championship football, owing more to some assault training based on dexterity of foot and mind. An important factor in all the unpleasantness was the refereeing of Mr Smith. He was always on the spot, and quick enough to see what went on, but wagging a finger at professionals is like using a feather for corporal punishment: it has no effect. If one or two players had been sent off, David Hollins, the Newcastle goalkeeper, might not have been carried off.

The ball was there to be caught. Dave could see that and moved accordingly to pluck Barry Bridges' 37th-minute corner kick from the air. The next thing he knew he was on the floor amid a pile of bodies. Not only had Chelsea equalised Newcastle's 26th-minute opening goal but the back of his head hurt like hell.

'I was led to believe it was an elbow from George Graham, as in the future manager of Arsenal,' says Dave. 'A lot of people went up for the ball, the elbow went into the back of my neck, and I just collapsed. It happened while I was in the air, which is a bit naughty as you're unlikely to be able to control how you fall. I remember looking up and seeing my brother John leaning over me but other than that I was too dazed to remember much. They stretchered me off, put Dave Hilley in goal until half-time, assessed me in the dressing room, then put me back on.'

They did what?

'They put me back on. We had no substitute goalkeeper and so I had to go back in goal. It finished 1-1, so I managed to keep a clean sheet in the second half. How, I really don't know. They were crazy times and player welfare wasn't what it is today. Goalkeepers in particular were targets, as we've discussed, and we weren't given any protection. That was the only way we knew, so we just got on with it.'

On the final whistle a quick-witted photographer had the presence of mind to take a picture of Dave and John walking from the pitch together, engrossed in conversation. Frozen in time, Dave looks well, while John appears unconcerned for his older brother's well-being. And yet, as Dave readily concedes, he's likely to have been suffering from concussion at the time. He only knows the moment happened because he's seen the photograph in question.

'They probably asked me at half-time if I was okay to continue and I would have said yes,' Dave surmises. 'That's exactly why a player is the last person you should put a question like that to, because in all likelihood they are in absolutely no fit state to decide.'

Seven days later, despite Marshall being fit again and available for selection, Dave kept his place for the visit of Arsenal to St James' Park. Newcastle lost 1-0 but their goalkeeper, showing no sign of any ill effects from the previous weekend, impressed.

Dave remained United's first choice throughout the remainder of October into November, a period that included important wins over Aston Villa (1-0) and Blackpool (2-0). Safe to say, however, that the camaraderie that often exists between goalkeepers, certainly in the case of Dave and Eric, wasn't really there when it came to Dave and Gordon Marshall.

How do we know this without Dave, ever the gent, having to say anything? Because, unbeknown to Dave, a thoroughly unhappy Marshall confronted Joe Harvey on several occasions about playing second fiddle, while also threatening to submit a transfer request. Good job he only had to suffer two months in the reserves rather than the better part of two years.

On 24 November Dave picked up a leg injury while playing for Wales in their 4-1 defeat to Scotland at Hampden Park, Glasgow, a night when the Scots ran riot and the Welsh, strangely for the class of 1965, failed to show.

Three days later, with Dave still unfit, Marshall returned for Newcastle's trip to Sheffield United, a match they lost 3-2. A goalkeeping showdown at St James' Park had been conveniently, if narrowly, averted.

By the time Dave was fit again, Marshall had recovered some kind of form, having underwhelmed for Newcastle in the 4-3 and 4-2 defeats to West Ham United and Aston Villa, respectively. Despite flirting with relegation throughout the remainder of the campaign, Dave failed to get another look-in at club level that season. As Orson Welles once said, 'Nobody ever gets justice. People only get good luck or bad luck.'

Not that Dave would see it that way. The man's too much of an optimist.

And yet, by the end of the 1965/66 season, even Dave could sense that a change of club might do him good.

'After a while, I did start to become affected by things that I saw and heard,' he admits. 'I'm talking about internal stuff such as people coming up to you saying, "Joe Harvey is after another goalkeeper." Or when team sheets go up on a Friday and your name isn't on it. You get to learn when perhaps you're not wanted anymore. And I reacted to that and decided I wanted to move. I didn't particularly want to go. As a family, we loved the area. That was important, as family always comes first. The children were at school and happy. We were settled. But, when it came to my day-to-day job, I really had no other option. If I wanted to make the most of whatever time I had left playing, then I had to leave.'

However, prior to making any decisions over where his club future might lie, Dave had another matter to attend to overseas. Once again, Brazil had qualified for the World Cup finals. Once again, they were after a European sparring partner to help get them in the groove for what lay ahead. Once again, a transatlantic phone call was made to the Football Association of Wales enquiring about the possibility of a friendly or two. One again, the Welsh said, 'You betcha' – or something to that effect.

'Of all the places that I played football in my career, Brazil would be the number one,' says Dave. 'We love our football here but out there it's a religion, as indeed it is in Italy. It comes above everything. The people are so friendly, so natural … and they didn't steal our shirts and towels from the beach this time! The poverty can be shocking but it doesn't seem to stop them smiling, and I found that approach to life infectious. Personally, I couldn't wait to go back. The only thing I was wondering about on the way out there was whether Brazil would field their first team or rest a few players. I mean, any Brazilian national team is going to be a force to be reckoned with, especially in those days, but there was a feeling one or two of them might be missing to keep a little in reserve for the finals, which were only a matter of weeks away.'

In the event, only one familiar face was absent from Brazil's starting XI as the teams lined up for the anthems inside Rio's Maracanã Stadium ahead of the first friendly on 14 May 1966 – and that was Pelé. With their sights set on lifting the World Cup for an unprecedented third time in a row, wrapping the planet's most gifted player in cotton wool kind of made sense. Otherwise it was business as usual from Gilmar in goal to Garrincha on the right side of attack. The 'A' team, in other words.

With time having finally caught up with the majority of their star names, including John Charles and Cliff Jones, Wales were always likely to find the going tough. And so it proved.

'The individuality of the Brazilian players was simply amazing,' Dave recollects. 'I'd been around a few years by then and thought I was pretty good at reading situations, but when you come up against players like that it's almost impossible to read them at all. They had so much natural flair and skill, the kind that almost can't be taught. Defending against that is always going to be extremely difficult. But you do your best.'

Dave did, indeed, do his best, producing several fine saves before Silva, deputising for Pelé, opened the scoring midway through the first half with a powerful shot from 20 yards out. Soon afterwards, Servílio doubled Brazil's lead. Although Ron Davies reduced the deficit just before half-time, Garrincha duly restored the home team's two-goal advantage after the break, placing an exquisite free kick just beyond Dave's reach.

On the final whistle, Gilmar once again made a beeline for Dave, just as he'd done four years previously. This time the pleasantries stopped at a handshake followed by a hug. No exchanging of jerseys. 'But then he already had one of mine, so why would he want another?' jokes Dave. 'I doubt he had a house big enough, anyway, to accommodate all the jerseys he'd swapped. He did, after all, play an awful lot of games for Brazil. I'm just glad I got to do it the once with him. That was enough for me.'

Four days later, Brazil fielded what amounted to their 'B' team in Belo Horizonte for the second friendly against Wales. On that occasion Dave stepped aside, giving Tony Millington the opportunity to show his mettle, which he duly did as the visitors slipped to a 1-0 defeat. In fact, Millington played so well that he held on to the goalkeeper's jersey for Wales's third and final match of their mini South American tour, a 2-0 defeat to Chile in Santiago.

All these years later, Dave remembers little if anything about Chile, which, at the time, was going through a period of major social and economic reform under its president Eduardo Frei Montalva. That's unlike Dave, who, besides great attention to detail, has the memory of an elephant. Then again, considering his uncertain future with Newcastle, it's not as if he didn't have other things on his mind at the time.

Get back to England. Spend time with the family. Watch the World Cup finals on television. Start searching for a new club. So went Dave's to-do list for the summer of 1966.

As it turned out, Dave's 11th Welsh cap, the 3-1 defeat in Rio that May, would prove to be his last. An international career that had started in Brazil ended up finishing in Brazil. At a time when countries played far fewer matches than they do today, and with Wales managers Jimmy Murphy and Dave Bowen choosing to rotate their goalkeepers rather than plump for just the one, 11 has to go down as pretty high cotton.

'Not bad for someone who didn't even know he qualified to play for his country,' as Dave puts it.

10

A PLACE WITHOUT A POSTCARD

'I don't have a short temper. I just have a quick reaction.' – Elizabeth Taylor

'Life is like a mountain railway
With an engineer that's brave
We must make the run successful
From the cradle to the grave
Heed the curves and hills and tunnels
Never falter, never fail
Keep your hand upon the throttle
And your eye upon the rail'

SO GO the opening lines to 'Life's Railway to Heaven' written way back in 1890 by M.E. Abbey and Charles Davis Tillman and performed over the years by just about every country, folk and gospel singer you can shake a stick at. It's a song that does exactly what it says on the tin, comparing the lifespan of a human being (and all we encounter along the way) to a journey by train.

'It was my mother's favourite and I've sung it so many times it has become one of mine too,' Johnny Cash once said in homage. 'Heed the curves and hills and tunnels. Isn't that what we all try and do?' Amen to that. And you don't argue with the gospel according to Johnny Cash.

The word 'friend' doesn't actually appear in the lyrics to 'Life's Railway to Heaven' but it's written large in the song's subtext (many of the acts that have recorded and performed it, Cash included, chose to do so surrounded by familiar faces). In our lifetimes we make friends through school, youth clubs, Scouts, Guides, college, university, backpacking, work, playing sport, watching sport, holidays, antenatal groups, social clubs, going to gigs, school runs, park runs, evening classes, volunteering and all manner of whatnot. The majority of those friends, for whatever reasons, will come and go along the way. Very few, if any, will be with us from cradle to grave. Schoolyard to grave, perhaps, yet even that's pushing it given the twists and turns, not to mention the odd derailment, that our respective trains will inevitably encounter throughout the years.

What Eric Gill and Dave Hollins have to this day, in other words, is something that's not only extremely rare but also incredibly precious to both men.

At the risk of making a colossal sweeping assertion, men and women tend to behave in markedly different ways when it comes to friendships. Women, more often than not, are just better at keeping in regular contact with their friends, be it in person, via email, letter, social media or over the phone. Men, on the other hand, can go for months, years even, without communicating with one another, only to slip straight back into the old groove once they finally do. When they're together, they make it count. That's not to say women don't. It's just that men have an inherent gift for picking up from where they left off many moons ago.

With that in mind, it's worth saying this is the point in our story where Eric and Dave really didn't see that much of each other. Which is no great surprise, given they were married fathers living busy lives at opposite ends of England. At some stage the opportunity to hook up again in person would arise – they knew that. The pair of them had too much history and respect for one another to let their friendship slide. For the time being, however, work and domesticity came first. Which, to be fair, it tended to do for the majority of men in 1960s Britain. No five-day stag trips to Las Vegas or golfing weekends with the lads in La Manga. Dave may have ventured out to an extent with Wales but, by and large, whether you were male or female, professional footballer or milkman, the world was a much smaller place, especially if your roots were working class.

Having arrived back on Tyneside from what would be his last Wales tour of duty all set to find a new club, Dave discovered to his surprise that Joe Harvey wasn't up for showing him the exit door at St James' Park quite yet. Four times he returned to Newcastle United's first team during the opening weeks of the 1966/67 league season, deputising again for Gordon Marshall. Yet his mind remained steadfast – at the first sight of land, he'd jump ship.

As it turned out, Dave's next port of call would prove to be about as landlocked as it's possible to be in England.

The 17-year-old Eric Gill practises his trade.

Eric receives his Army Cup winner's medal from King George VI and Queen Elizabeth, April 1950.

Dave Hollins in conversation with Billy Lane, manager of Brighton & Hove Albion.

Brighton's rock. Eric in his prime as a goalkeeper during the 1950s.

At home with the Gills – Eric plays with his son Steve as wife Ida looks on.

Eric on Brighton's treatment table being tended to by club trainer Joe Wilson.

Brighton's 1957/58 promotion winning team with Eric standing centre, bottle of bubbly in hand.

Brighton line up for the 1958/59 season, with Eric and Dave stood middle row, fourth from left and fourth from right, respectively.

Eric fends off the Stoke City attack at Brighton's Goldstone Ground, April 1959.

Eric on the eve of the 1959/60 season, his last as a Brighton player.

Dave prepares to keep goal for Brighton against Preston North End in the fifth round of the FA Cup, February 1960.

Dave and his younger brother John, combs at the ready.

Dave flies to his left to make a save in Newcastle United's 4-2 win away against Blackburn Rovers, April 1961.

Dave, third from left, back row, lines up alongside his Newcastle team-mates during the 1961/62 season.

Dave in action for Newcastle against Scunthorpe United. (Paul Joannou Archive)

Brian Clough gets the better of Dave at St James' Park, scoring for Sunderland against Newcastle in October 1962. (Paul Joannou Archive)

Dave follows Stan Anderson out of the tunnel at St James' Park, November 1963.

Dave on international duty for Wales at Ninian Park, Cardiff.

Eric leads the Guildford City team onto the field at Joseph's Road.

Dave and brother John walk together from the pitch following Newcastle's 1-1 draw with Chelsea, September 1965. (courtesy of NUFC)

Dave snuffs out a Liverpool attack at St James' Park, October 1965. (Paul Joannou Archive)

Dave, second from right on the back row, lines up alongside his Mansfield Town team-mates, 1968/69.

Ex-Brighton player Gordon Smith joins Dave on the field at the Amex Stadium before Brighton's game against Newcastle, November 2021. (courtesy of Paul Hazlewood)

'Absolute concentration' – Eric and Dave adopt their game faces at Denton Island Indoor Bowls Club, February 2022. (courtesy of Paul Hazlewood)

'That's true friendship' – Eric and Dave share a joke in their bowling attire. (courtesy of Paul Hazlewood)

'Joe asked me into his office one day and started talking about Tommy Cummings, who had played for Burnley for many years and was now managing Mansfield Town,' Dave recalls. 'Joe said they were interested in me and asked if I'd like to move, to which I said yeah. I went down there with Jackie, met up with Tommy Cummings, had a look around the ground and was introduced to some of the players. And I thought, *This will do me*. Field Mill was a little different to St James' Park in terms of size but the people around the place seemed to be smiling and the place clearly had a heart. Mansfield were a Third Division club that hadn't really achieved much over the years, the sort of old-fashioned outfit where you're told to take care of your kit because you only get one set of everything each year. But they said the right things – "We're out to build a better team" and what have you – and clearly wanted to go in the right direction. Then they asked if I'd sign.'

Any reservations about dropping from the First to the Third Division, not to mention leaving the family's beloved, albeit rented, Newcastle townhouse behind?

'No, not at all. We'd had a marvellous six years up there and I'd got the chance to play for what I still regard as one of the most wonderful football clubs in the world. It had been an honour being their goalkeeper, having the opportunity to test myself against the very best strikers in the country. Then there'd been the greatest honour of all … having Stanley Matthews score against me! We were away to Stoke City and I had Alf McMichael in front of me at left-back, who usually played a decent game against Stan. Anyway, Stan came up and went straight through Alf with a dummy, leaving him with only me to beat.

I pushed him out wide on to an angle and mistakenly thought, *I've got you here.* All of a sudden, he swivelled his hips and bang – the ball was in the back of the net. He must have been about 50 at the time but the skill of the man was immense. He had so much respect at that time that you rarely saw anybody dare tackle him. Funny, isn't it, that one of my most treasured memories should involve conceding a goal? But you have to respect a person like that, someone of such high skill and a gentleman with it. Six eventful years with plenty of highs and one or two lows. But you move on.'

On 25 February 1967, Dave made his debut for Mansfield Town – nicknamed The Stags – in a 2-1 defeat away to Oxford United, ironically one of the clubs Eric had come up against on several occasions for Guildford City prior to them joining the Football League in place of the doomed Accrington Stanley. The following weekend he made his bow at Field Mill in front of a healthy 12,815 attendance, keeping Bristol Rovers' strikers at bay in a 2-0 win.

Just as Gordon Marshall had unseated Dave as the regular number one at St James' Park, so Dave rapidly came to elbow poor Alan Humphreys out of the frame at Mansfield. Such is life when there can only ever be one player of your position in the team.

* * *

Draw a line on a map from Brighton to Newcastle upon Tyne and you'll discover Mansfield really isn't that much further from the former as it is the latter. And yet, in terms of character, the place has far more in common with the north-east of England than the deep south, built as it was on heavy industry rather than fresh air and tourism. When Dave arrived in Mansfield, the town still danced to the tune of the mining industry and the rich coal seams beneath the north Nottinghamshire soil, which kept thousands of local men in employment. In 1967 pits were opening in the area rather than closing, bringing a mass migration of miners from other parts of Britain, including Scotland and, ironically, north-east England – economic migrants who, inevitably, brought with them their love of association football. The place had work which meant people had money, plenty of which crossed over the turnstiles at Field Mill. Boom time, so it was, even if the ever-present dangers of mining lay quite literally at the root of that prosperity.

Like Newcastle, Mansfield also had some pretty spectacular countryside on its doorstep, which the Hollins family wasted no time exploring.

'You were right in the middle of lots of counties such as Derbyshire and Yorkshire where there was plenty to see and do,' says Dave. 'On Sundays we'd take the children on drives to places like the Peak District and Chatsworth House, exploring all this rolling countryside and the little towns hidden amongst it. Mansfield itself wasn't a town of ice creams, candyfloss and picture postcards like Brighton but the people were so friendly, equally as friendly as anything we'd encountered in the north-east. It was a good area and we loved living there. In fact we still keep in contact with quite a few friends from that time.'

Mansfield Town finished a solid ninth in the Third Division that season, with Dave very nearly becoming the club's first-ever player to win international recognition along the way. Without Gary Sprake for their Home International Championship fixture against Northern Ireland in Belfast on 12 April 1967, Wales once again turned to Dave to do the honours. However, hours before the call-up came through Dave had been declared unfit to play for Mansfield at Swindon Town, having suffered a thigh strain against Swansea Town the previous Saturday. If he couldn't play for The Stags on the Tuesday then he certainly couldn't play for Wales 24 hours later. The answer had to be thanks but no thanks, and a small yet significant piece of Mansfield Town history slipped through his fingers.

That summer, Tommy Cummings, the man responsible for bringing Dave to Field Mill, was appointed as Aston's Villa's new manager, leaving the Mansfield position vacant. *Here we go again*, thought Dave, mindful of the managerial merry-go-round that had left him fearing – correctly, as it emerged – for his first-team place at Newcastle United a few years previously. Fortunately, he needn't have worried.

'We got hold of this chap called Tommy Eggleston, who had been a coach at Everton under the management of Harry Catterick,' says Dave. 'I took to him straightaway because, as a tactician, he was absolutely brilliant. His attention to detail really was second to none. Up until then our standard of play had been slightly agricultural, let's just say. The pitches in those days in the Third Division, particularly the one at Field Mill, were often very muddy. Playing controlled football on them was out of the question. Playing on muddy pitches without any real tactics will only get you so far. Playing on muddy pitches with your tactics sorted out – well, that's a different matter. You've got a better chance.'

Even so, Mansfield took a mighty long time getting into gear under Eggleston. In his first full season in charge, 1967/68, they finished 20th of 24 clubs in the Third Division. Had Peterborough United not been deducted 19 points for making irregular bonus payments to their players, then Mansfield would have finished 21st and been relegated. In the first round of the FA Cup they were hammered 5-1 away by part-timers Tow Law Town of the Northern League. Many managers would count themselves fortunate to survive that ignominy, let alone an entire season of below-par performances.

As for Dave, he did what he could to stem the tide, never conceding more than three goals in any one league match while managing to keep nine clean sheets, shutouts or whatever your shorthand happens to be for when a goalie goes unbeaten throughout an entire match – not a bad record for a keeper in a struggling team. It would in all likelihood have been ten, save for the events that took place midway through the second half of Mansfield's home match against Gillingham on Saturday, 2 December 1967.

Picture this. For 70 long minutes Mansfield had swarmed around Gillingham's goal – rattling the woodwork, having shots saved by the visiting keeper, having shots cleared off the line, having shots get stuck in the mud, etc. The kind of luck, or lack of it, you tend to associate with a football team at the wrong end of the league. Out of the blue, Gillingham suddenly break away. Their centre-forward, Bill Brown, finds himself in yards of space without a Mansfield defender in sight. Everyone on the field besides Brown, Dave included, stops, waiting for referee David Laing to blow his whistle for offside. Only he doesn't. Brown sticks the ball into the net, Laing awards the goal ... and Field Mill goes into meltdown.

'The chap ran through in an offside position, yards and yards offside, and I stood there naturally thinking play was about to stop,' Dave recalls of the circumstances surrounding the only sending-off of his entire career. 'How on earth the linesman didn't see it, I just don't know. Everybody stood still, including me. I know they say you should always play to the referee's whistle but this was the most clear-cut offside you could ever wish to see, so I automatically stopped. It was so obvious. And yet he gave it. I went mad. I wasn't the only one but I went really mad and was sent off for foul and abusive language. I'm not a foul and abusive person but, when something is so wrong and you're absolutely astounded that somebody can make such a stupid mistake, then anyone can occasionally lose it. And I lost it. My wife was in a playground a couple of miles away with the children and she could hear the crowd from there. When I got home, she said, "What on earth happened?" I said, "Well, I got sent off." It had never happened before and it never happened again. Off I went and, inevitably, we ended up losing 1-0.'

A couple of days after the regular 1967/68 league season had finished, 160-odd miles due south of Mansfield, a crowd of around 600 people gathered in the teeming rain at Joseph's Road to watch Guildford City take on a West Ham United XI in Eric Gill's benefit match. Once upon a time, when the average wage for a professional footballer was small potatoes compared to today, benefit matches (sometimes known as testimonials) were a vital means of harvesting some hard cash at the end of one's career for whatever lay ahead. Eric, an ex-professional footballer playing for a semi-professional club on what amounted to professional wages, hadn't received a benefit game at Brighton & Hove Albion. He did, however, already have an established business to fall back on. Money wasn't tight, in other words. Nevertheless, with a family to support and hotel overheads to take care of, every pound still counted. The benefit match at Joseph's Road would, hopefully, take care of some of those overheads.

High-profile opposition and good weather – that's all any player fortunate enough to be honoured with a benefit match prayed for when the big day came around. On that front Eric scored 50 per cent. Although West Ham were missing two of their celebrated England World Cup winners from 1966 (Bobby Moore and Geoff Hurst), the third, Martin Peters, did make the trip to Guildford alongside several other first-teamers and up-and-coming youngsters such as Billy Bonds, Trevor Brooking, Frank Lampard (senior) and Harry Redknapp. The kind of team that, if you lived in deepest Surrey and followed football in 1968, you probably would have paid to see on a Monday night providing the weather was good, which, unfortunately, it wasn't.

'It rained all bloody day and killed the crowd,' says Eric ruefully. 'On a good night there might have been two or three thousand there. But I still enjoyed it, meeting all the people who did come. I distinctly remember somebody passing a hat around in the crowd and they were all putting money in. Isn't that a lovely thing to do? I got some money from it, which was nice, but the memories are just as important. And what a lovely thing for West Ham to do.'

The West Ham United connection had come about something like this. By now Eric and Ida's sons, Steve and Malcolm, were long past the days of being babysat by Dave and Jackie. In fact Steve had turned into a pretty useful footballer himself. Aged 15 he'd already appeared alongside Eric on several occasions, playing centre-forward for Guildford's midweek team made up of rookies and reserves. At 16 West Ham offered him an apprenticeship, which he accepted. Over the weeks and months that followed, Eric, brought increasingly into the east London club's orbit, formed a mutual appreciation society with Ron Greenwood, United's manager at the time, which resulted in the future England boss offering to bring a team to Joseph's Road to play in Eric's benefit match.

'When my son went there, Ron and I used to have words while we were standing out on the touchline together at matches,' remembers Eric. 'He knew of me. In fact, I seem to recall him saying that we'd once played against each other. He was very good to me, and I'm not just saying that because he arranged to bring a team down to Guildford for my match. He was very good to me because I was an ex-pro. Whenever he saw me at a match at West Ham, he'd always invite me into the directors' box – "Eric, you come with me," and off we'd go. As far as I was concerned, he was a really, really nice guy.'

'Dad didn't actually play in his testimonial match because he wanted to be part of the crowd,' adds Steve Gill. 'He wanted to be there for the people, welcoming them in, sorting out the raffle and all those sorts of things. Ron Greenwood was very good because he took me along as a substitute, even though he'd selected a team of established pros and I was only an apprentice. He brought me on at half-time for John Sissons, which is amazing in itself because John Sissons was quite a player. It finished 4-1 to West Ham and I managed to score one of the goals. Harry Redknapp put over a cross and I got on the end of it with my left foot. Afterwards I said to dad, "Did you see my goal?" And he said, "No, I didn't, I was going round with the raffle tickets!" That night meant a lot to me – being there for dad, scoring a goal, being surrounded by all those top players. It's something I'll never, ever forget.'

* * *

'8-1. 8 bloody 1. 8-1 … to Brighouse!'

So begins Gordon Ottershaw's splendid rant towards the start of *Golden Gordon*, the penultimate episode of the *Ripping Yarns* television comedy series written by Michael Palin and Terry Jones of Monty Python fame, which aired in Britain during the mid-to-late 1970s.

Set in 1935, Gordon is a supporter of Barnstoneworth United, a once proud football club that hasn't won a home match at its Sewage Works ground in years. After each miserable defeat he goes home and, while his long-suffering wife looks on, destroys various pieces of furniture in frustration. The Ottershaws have a son called Barnstoneworth (middle name United) who, parrot-fashion, recites the names of entire teams from the club's better days. Take, for example, the Yorkshire Premier League cup side from 1922:

'Hagerty F., Hagerty R., Tompkins, Noble, Carrick, Robson, Crapper, Dewhurst, McIntyre, Treadmore, Davitt.'

Or the reserve team from the 1922 Yorkshire Premier League:

'Bolton, Roberts, Carter, Sidney K., Tatwell, Mason, Manningham, Bailey, Boswell, Dobkins, O'Grady.'

Driven to the point of insanity by his team of 'useless, useless bastards' and with the club on the verge of being sold to the Arthur Foggen Scrap Corporation for redevelopment, Gordon sets out on a crusade to reunite the great Barnstoneworth team of 1922 for what's due to be United's last-ever match, a cup tie against Denley Moor Academicals. His crusade comes up trumps. The veterans win the match 8-1. Cock-a-hoop, Gordon rushes home and, aided and abetted by Mrs Ottershaw and Barnstoneworth, smashes up the living room in delight.

There are people in north Nottinghamshire today who, like young Barnstoneworth, can name the Mansfield Town team of 1968/69 at the drop of a hat and without blinking:

Hollins, Pate, Hopkinson, Quigley, Boam, Waller, Keeley, Sharkey, Ledger, Roberts, Goodfellow.

The 11 men who started every single one of Mansfield's ties during their remarkable run to the latter stages of that season's FA Cup competition.

In August 1968, The Stags were by no stretch of the imagination in the same hole that Barnstoneworth had found themselves back in 1935. They won the odd home match. No proposed sale to a scrap merchant loomed large. As bitterly disappointing as the 1967/68 campaign had been, their supporters weren't at the stage where they would arrive home from Field Mill and destroy items of furniture – well, maybe the odd one or two were.

Even so, bells and whistles were the last things on the minds of anyone connected with the club as the 1968/69 season got underway with a 2-1 away win against, of all teams, Brighton & Hove Albion. By the time the first round of the FA Cup came around in mid-November, Mansfield had slipped into the lower reaches of the Third Division. The club badly needed a lift and duly got it with a 4-1 win over Tow Law Town, the very same Tow Low Town that had thrashed them 5-1 in the first round of the same competition the previous season.

Ask any chairman or secretary in the third or fourth tiers of English football what their ideal FA Cup scenario would be and they will almost certainly say reaching the third round of the competition and being drawn against a big club either home or away. That applies as much today as it did in 1968. The only difference is that back then the FA Cup really, really mattered.

Besides Christmas and birthdays, no other date on the calendar was more important to a large percentage of the English and Welsh male population than FA Cup Final day (sorry ladies, but we're talking bygone times here). Instead of resting their best players and fielding herds of relative unknowns, top-flight clubs always put out their strongest teams, regardless of who the opposition were. Unless you considered yourself an England World Cup winner, playing in an FA Cup Final at Wembley was the high point of every domestic professional footballer's career. Even better if you got to win the thing.

Standing between Mansfield and a potential money-spinning third-round tie were Rotherham United, also a Third Division club. The match, played at Rotherham's former home of Millmoor (situated, ironically, next door to a scrap merchant's yard), finished 2-2 in controversial circumstances, both United goals being given despite a linesman flagging for offside for the first and Dave being barged to the ground in the build-up to the second.

Forty-eight hours later Mansfield gained revenge of sorts when Bob Ledger's first-half strike gave them victory by a solitary goal in the replay.

And so to round three – the biggie, the money-spinner, the one where players and fans alike live the dream by going to Anfield or Old Trafford or Highbury or White Hart Lane. Sheffield United of the Second Division at home wasn't quite in the script but that's the hand Mansfield were dealt. Once again, The Stags prevailed, this time without the need of a replay, coming from a goal down to score twice in two second-half minutes in front of 17,430 seriously pumped-up spectators.

Surely now, with fewer and fewer clubs involved at each stage of the competition, there was every chance of Anfield or Old Trafford or Highbury or White Hart Lane in round four? Think again. Southend United of the Fourth Division at home, to be played on Saturday, 25 January 1969. Not exactly a glamour tie, from either a Mansfield or a Southend perspective.

'The one big advantage we had of being drawn at home throughout that cup run was the state of our pitch,' says Dave. 'That particular winter happened to be a really bad one, which affected pitches everywhere. It's just that ours seemed to be affected more so! The surface became very thick, very muddy. You couldn't really play on it, which made it a great leveller. We sort of got used to it, as much as you can get used to playing on mud, whereas other teams needed a bit of time to adjust – providing, that is, they were able to at all. If they couldn't, then that was our job more or less done for us.'

Once again, Mansfield had to come from behind against a dogged Southend, with Nick Sharkey equalising shortly after half-time before Dudley Roberts headed what proved to be the winner in the 77th minute. As the visitors gave it one last roll of the dice, so Dave proved himself equal to Gary Moore's close-range header and a powerful rising shot by Ian Hamilton, finger-tipped away at the expense of a corner. Fourteen years after turning professional, Mansfield's goalie was finally experiencing the magic of the cup for himself.

'A couple of years beforehand, my brother John had played for Chelsea against Tottenham in the final at the old Wembley Stadium and there had been this fantastic family gathering to mark the occasion,' Dave recalls. 'Mansfield were nowhere near Wembley at that stage but it's nice when you're progressing through the rounds and seeing what it's doing to the fans, the sheer amount of jubilation it creates.

'I hate to say it but the FA Cup is a third-rate competition these days. They've totally destroyed it. The final used to be one of the most important days in the entire year, the traditional climax to the domestic season. Now it's just buried among a mountain of other Premier League fixtures with a 5.30pm kick-off. It doesn't have anything like the effect on people that it used to, and I think that's a crying shame.'

It was at this point that the weather really began to play havoc not only with Mansfield's FA Cup run but also their entire season. Having reached the fifth round, the club were now having to postpone league fixtures to accommodate cup matches. On top of that, the cup matches were also being put back due to snow, which would melt, adding to the cake mix that Mansfield's pitch was fast resembling. Then it would snow again. Then it would melt again. And repeat. To quote Town historian Paul Taylor: 'It got to the stage where there was more sand on our pitch than Skegness beach.'

In the draw for the fifth round, Mansfield were paired against West Ham United at Field Mill. Five times the tie was postponed, which if anything only upped the sense of expectation prior to the match finally taking place on the evening of Wednesday, 26 February.

'I've heard since that certain West Ham players were absolutely shitting themselves on the coach on the way to the ground because they didn't fancy it,' chortles Dave. 'They knew the conditions wouldn't suit their style of play. They knew the pitch would be waterlogged. They knew the crowd would be right in their faces under the floodlights. We knew West Ham played a passing game – that's why Tommy Eggleston told Nick Sharkey, our striker, to stay within a yard of Bobby Moore at all times. "Stick to him and do not allow him to pass the ball," Tommy said. He basically told Nick that his job wasn't to score goals but to do a marking job instead. It was an amazing tactical ploy. And that's what won us the match.'

Besides marking Bobby Moore out of the game, Nick Sharkey also managed to score, dispossessing West Ham's Scottish international goalkeeper Bobby Ferguson in the 49th minute to put Mansfield 3-0 up. And that's the way it finished. Whatever West Ham attempted to try to get back into the game, Town always seemed a step ahead of them with Stuart Boam, their young centre-half, doing an admirable job of marshalling Geoff Hurst. On the one occasion when England's 1966 World Cup Final hat-trick hero did threaten Mansfield's goal, Dave was out quickly to narrow the angle and beat his shot away.

John Peet of the *Nottingham Evening Post* found himself vying for space in Field Mill's press box with the great and the good of Fleet Street. He wrote:

> West Ham United, complete with World Cup stars, staggered before the onslaught of lowly Mansfield Town at Field Mill last night and finally returned to London well beaten while the home fans celebrated a piece of soccer history – The Stags' arrival in the FA Cup quarter-finals for the first time.

Peet was right but also slightly off. The Mansfield versus West Ham match (along with Leicester City's tie against Liverpool) had been postponed so many times that the draw for the semi-finals had already taken place, pitting:

Manchester City v Everton
West Bromwich Albion v Mansfield Town or
Leicester City

Beat Leicester City at home on Saturday, 8 March and
Mansfield's players and fans would be heading up the
recently completed M1 motorway three weeks later to
take on the reigning FA Cup holders at Hillsborough,
Sheffield, for a place in the final. For a club that should
by rights have been relegated from the Third Division the
previous season, that's pretty remarkable.

'I don't recall us as players getting too carried away
with the prospect of being in the semi-finals, although
the supporters by that time were going crazy, as you can
imagine,' Dave maintains. 'As far as we were concerned
– well, certainly in my case – I was just focusing on the
next game, which, in terms of the cup, was Leicester. They
certainly weren't going to be pushovers, being in the old
First Division as they were and having a very promising
up-and-coming young goalkeeper in their ranks by the
name of Peter Shilton. But on that pitch and having just
beaten West Ham and all their World Cup winners, I
think we fancied our chances against anyone.'

In 1969 man went to the Moon for the very first time.
Richard Nixon went into the White House as the 37th
President of the United States of America. The Beatles
went on to the roof of their Apple Records headquarters
in Savile Row, London, to give the band's last-ever public
performance. And Peter Shilton went to Field Mill and
broke Mansfield hearts with a towering performance
that sent Leicester City through to the semi-finals of
the FA Cup.

The record books show that Rod Fern's 58th-minute
header gave the visitors the slenderest of victories over The
Stags. It was, however, the future England goalkeeper's

man-of-the-match performance that dominated the headlines.

'It was a game we could have won quite easily – well, not easily, but we could have won if it hadn't been for Peter,' insists Dave. 'He was so assured throughout in his positional play. He was a lovely, clean kicker of the ball. And he made some very good saves. I rated him that day and forever afterwards. At the end I wanted to do a "Gilmar" and swap shirts with him but, in the melee, I never got the chance. And that, unfortunately, was the end of our cup run. Even to this day, I still believe it was one of the greatest cup runs by a little club in the history of the competition. It's something I'm very proud to be associated with.'

'The one thing which does annoy me is that, when people talk about FA Cup giant-killers, nobody ever mentions the Mansfield Town team of 1968/69,' says Stags historian Paul Taylor. 'You always get Hereford versus Newcastle [from 1972] and Sutton beating Coventry [from 1989] and what have you because they were captured on television, whereas none of our matches were. We made the papers at the time – "Hammers Are Hammered" and all that kind of thing. And the *Sunday Mirror*, for what it's worth, made us the winners of their "Giant-killer Cup". But that's not much to show for something that brought so much joy to the town. There is that one claim to fame, though, the fact the same 11 players started every single game throughout that entire cup run. I like that.'

Who, in case you needed reminding, were:

Hollins, Pate, Hopkinson, Quigley, Boam, Waller, Keeley, Sharkey, Ledger, Roberts, Goodfellow.

Barnstoneworth United, eat your heart out.

With their FA Cup endeavours at an end, Mansfield had a lot of ground to make up in the league that season due to postponements. In April alone they played no fewer than 11 matches, three of them coming within the space of just four days. Almost inevitably, such an intense schedule took its toll on some tired legs. In the end The Stags finished the season in 15th place, significantly lower than many around Field Mill felt they would had the spring fixture pile-up not occurred. Still, you can't have everything. Over half a century later it's the FA Cup run that still gets talked about in the avenues and alleyways of Mansfield, not their league position.

The 1968/69 campaign proved to be Dave's last full season at Mansfield Town. Later that year Tommy Eggleston brought Graham Brown to Field Mill, a goalkeeper who had plied his trade in non-league football yet would go on to have a varied career at numerous professional clubs in England and Wales as well as North America. Dave and Graham ended up sharing the jersey for two-thirds of the 1969/70 season, which included another decent run in the FA Cup, with Dave playing in the first, second and third rounds against Bury, Shrewsbury Town and Barnsley, respectively.

By the time Leeds United dumped them out of the competition at the fifth-round stage in early February, Dave had left Field Mill (at least for the time being) and embarked on what would be his last spell of football at the very highest level, one he'd ultimately find as enjoyable as it was unexpected.

'I wasn't starting every game at Mansfield by then and I think I'd already begun looking around to see if there was anything else on the horizon,' says Dave. 'Then word came through that Nottingham Forest had a goalkeeping crisis. Alan Hill, their regular keeper, was injured, and Peter Grummitt, who was the back-up, couldn't play either for whatever reason. So I was asked, "Do you want to go there on loan?" This was Nottingham Forest prior to Brian Clough guiding them to European Cup glory but they were still a good First Division side. So I said, "Yes I do," and ended up playing the last ten or so games of the season for them.'

Which included another encounter with younger brother John.

'We'd played against each other that one time beforehand when he was at Chelsea and I was at Newcastle. He was still at Chelsea but all of a sudden there I was keeping goal for Nottingham Forest. That first game had finished 1-1 and that's exactly how the second one finished as well. That period at Nottingham Forest, brief though it was, was a lovely end to my career and getting to play against John again was the icing on the cake. It wasn't over quite yet but that was my last hurrah at what you might call an elite level. And I had great fun there. In the Third Division you've got to be so alert because players will shoot from anywhere. That didn't happen in the First Division, where they'd look to create spaces, then shoot. That was about the only slight difference I found in terms of having to adapt to a higher level of football again. But I felt I did okay.'

There was never any prospect of Dave's loan spell at the City Ground turning into anything more permanent – with two first-rate goalkeepers already on the club's payroll, he knew that. On Friday, 10 April 1970, Nottingham Forest brought the curtain down on their season with a 1-0 home win over Ipswich Town and Dave returned to being a Mansfield Town player. A few days later a postcard arrived at the Hollins household from Nottingham Forest's manager, Matt Gillies.

'It was a postcard thanking me for my services to Nottingham Forest,' Dave remembers. 'I thought it was a lovely gesture. That was the old-fashioned way of doing things. These people, they were different. It was their way of showing respect, by putting something down in writing. Recently I was going through some old documents and I came across a letter that my brother John had received from Joe Mears, Chelsea's chairman, when he'd just signed his first contract with the club at the age of 16 or 17. It was a lovely letter, beautifully worded. This postcard from Matt Gillies was the same. He wanted to thank me personally for everything I'd done, and I appreciated that. I've still got the postcard to this day.'

'It's nice when you get thanked for your efforts,' adds Eric. 'It's like when I had my benefit game at Guildford – they didn't have to do that for me. Goalkeepers often get forgotten about in football. We know how important we are, but not everyone else does. Strikers and midfielders get the glory and recognition because they get the goals. But goalkeepers are just as important, if not more so. We don't go looking for thanks – we just get on with our job – but a little thanks, when it does come along, is always appreciated.'

11

TIME, GENTLEMEN

'It's tough to find an encore.' – Eugene Cernan
(the last man, as of now, to walk on the Moon)

'WHAT'S THAT expression, the one you sometimes hear people say when they get towards the end of their careers?' asks Eric Gill.

You're a long time retired?

'That's the one! Well it's true. You don't want to go too soon, do you? If you like doing what you do, then you should carry on doing it for as long as possible. You'll know when it's the right time to stop.'

Unlike many footballers facing the prospect of retirement, Eric already knew what he was going to do with his life when the final whistle blew. He had, after all, been a hotelier for many years in tandem with his football career. But that's not to say he didn't want to squeeze every last ounce out of his semi-professional existence with Guildford City.

Seven months after the West Ham United XI benefit, Eric played his last match in anger when, responding to a goalkeeping injury crisis, he held the fort for Guildford's Southern League Premier Division fixture at Hillingdon Borough on 28 December 1968. By that time he'd long since known the end was nigh.

'When I was about 37, which would have been a year or so before my benefit match, Albert Tennant and me sat down and had a little chat together,' Eric recalls. 'Albert was the one who had signed me and he was still there when I left. We just gelled, me and him. A lovely man. Anyway, he goes, "Look, Eric, you've had a good run, but I think it's time you put your boots away now." And he was right. When you're in your mid-to-late thirties you're not the man you were in your mid-to-late twenties. Time starts catching up with you. So I had my benefit and then I finished. They could have just got rid of me but they kept me on for a year, which was a nice gesture. After that I did a bit of scouting for them, which they paid me for. And then that was that.'

They say boxers are the first to know when to quit but the last to admit it. The same adage can apply to association football goalkeepers, whose careers tend to last longer than outfield players as it is.

'There's something Eric used to say, which I totally agree with him on,' says Dave. 'It went like this: "When balls are going past you that never used to go past you, then it's time. Mate, you've reached the end of the line." When you look at it that way, the last couple of years of your career, you're done. You're just playing on while reality bites, wondering when to pull the plug. I guess there are many goalkeepers, maybe even the majority, who've experienced that feeling.

Not that we'd ever openly admit it, certainly not at the time.'

Having returned to Mansfield Town in April 1970 from his loan spell at Nottingham Forest, Dave was pleasantly surprised to discover yet another club waiting in the wings for his services. During the early years of his professional career at Brighton & Hove Albion, Dave had often come up against Jimmy Melia, the diminutive livewire at the heart of Liverpool's midfield. In November 1968, Melia joined Fourth Division Aldershot as the club's player-coach, assuming the position of manager five months later aged just 31. On hearing Dave was available, Jimmy got in touch and promptly signed him on a permanent transfer in June 1970.

'I'd always had a lot of time for Jimmy,' says Dave. 'He was one of those players who enjoyed joking and talking to goalkeepers during matches, the sort of player I had a real affinity for. You can always tell a lot about a person from how they dress. Jimmy had his very own way of dressing, very flamboyant. His shoes alone were unbelievable. Later on he became quite famous as Brighton's manager, leading them to the [1983] FA Cup Final at Wembley in his white disco shoes. He was another of those Harry Redknapp types, only classier. But he also had his own style of play. Everything was about the ball. I knew training at Aldershot under him would be fun, creative, five-a-sides, not endless cross-country runs. When I heard he'd come in for me, I didn't have to think twice.'

There was, though, another reason why Dave was keen to put pen to paper with Aldershot – it meant he'd be going home.

'That, in many ways, was the most exciting part for me,' he admits. 'Aldershot is only a few miles from Guildford where I'd been brought up. I'd loved our time in the north of England but the south was where my heart, and the rest of the family, was. We found a plot of land, had our very own house built, and while that was happening lived with my mum and dad. It was like things had gone full circle. You don't want to spend too long with your mum and dad when you're a married man in your thirties with a family, but while we were there it was very nice. And it was good to be back in the area.'

On a less positive note, Dave's form was starting to concern him. He was still only 32, relatively young in goalkeeping terms. But there'd been an awful lot of wear and tear to contend with over those years. Had Dave played in the modern era – on lush and level pitches instead of muddy, pockmarked cow fields, protected by referees from malicious centre-forwards, tended to by qualified physiotherapists instead of well-meaning amateurs – then there's every chance his career would have continued unabated.

Instead he found himself stalked by an ominous voice inside his head reciting Eric's 'dying of the light' goalkeeping proverb: 'When balls are going past you that never used to go past you, then it's time. Mate, you've reached the end of the line'.

Were balls now going past Dave that never used to?

'Absolutely, yeah,' he admits.

He'd had a good run but, like Eric a few years beforehand, the time to put the boots away was approaching.

Dave's Aldershot swansong lasted just 17 league and cup matches spanning three months, all too brief yet long enough to include a memorable encounter against the player he still rates as the finest of them all. Step forward Mr George Best.

'We were drawn against Manchester United at home in the League Cup, as it was then known,' remembers Dave. 'All their big players were there – Denis Law, Bobby Charlton, George Best, Nobby Stiles – except for Alex Stepney, the goalkeeper. We kicked downhill in the first half and, I'm not joking, we could have been at least three or four goals up. But Jimmy Rimmer, who was in their goal instead of Alex, played out of this world. Just before half-time Jimmy threw the ball to George. Off he went on this run that cut through all of us, including me, before sticking the ball in the net. It was just astonishing. If it hadn't been for George, I don't think they would have won the tie. He completely took over. Nobody wins a football match single-handedly but that's about as close as I've ever seen it happen. My brother John always said George was the greatest player of all time and I would wholeheartedly agree with that.'

Coming from an international team-mate of John Charles, who went toe to toe with Pelé and Garrincha, not to mention just about all the greats of the domestic game from the late 1950s to the very early 1970s, that's saying something.

For the record, Dave faced Best on three separate occasions over the course of his career. The goal he conceded at Aldershot's Recreation Ground in the second round of the League Cup that September evening was the only time the fifth Beatle, as Best was sometimes known, managed to get the better of him. There's many a member of the goalkeepers' union from those distant days who would gladly take that.

On Friday, 30 October 1970, under the floodlights at Layer Road, home to Colchester United, Dave pulled on his string gloves for the very last time as a professional. Aldershot lost 5-2, a result that prompted Melia to axe several players for the following weekend's home match against Workington. Dave was one of them. The Saturday prior to the Colchester defeat he'd been rock solid in the 3-0 home win over Barrow. Whoever came up with the old sporting cliché of 'you're only as good as your last game' just might have had the position of goalkeeper in mind.

As far as all parties were concerned, there were no hard feelings over the premature ending. 'Aldershot were alright about it and I think Jimmy was fine, though maybe a bit disappointed underneath that things hadn't worked out as they might,' says Dave. 'Eric and I both met up with Jimmy at a Brighton reunion dinner many years later, a double celebration to mark the anniversary of the 1958 promotion year and the 1983 FA Cup Final. It was lovely to see him again. And you know what? He was no different. He hadn't changed one bit. He still had his dancing shoes on!'

Over what remained of the 1970/71 season, Dave played a dozen or so matches for the Southern League outfit Romford – one of them, irony of ironies, away against Guildford City at Joseph's Road – before calling it a day, full stop. The rage, not to mention the light, had died. It was, so he recalls, 'then just a question of picking up my trade and carrying on with my life'.

And therein lies another reason why Dave was so keen to return south to his roots.

'My dad had insisted that my elder brother and I learn a trade before we ever got round to kicking a football professionally,' he says. 'Off I'd gone to Guildford Technical College to learn about interior decorating so that, when the time came for me to retire from football, I could start my own little business. And that's exactly what I did – interior decorating, specialising in quite expensive wallpapers. My reasoning about getting back to Guildford and the stockbroker belt was if you couldn't make money there, then you couldn't make money anywhere. That final transfer to Aldershot just brought us back a little bit earlier than we'd anticipated.'

Today, the concept of a professional footballer – one with considerable top-flight experience in England as well as international pedigree – switching trades to interior decorating almost overnight is unthinkable bordering on laughable. Imagine Wayne Rooney, Steven Gerrard or Petr Čech turning up on your doorstep in their overalls, paintbrushes and rollers at the ready. With some prudent financial advice, the average Premier League footballer need never work again on retiring from the game. Which is just as well in terms of that paintbrushes and rollers analogy because Wayne, Steve and Petr would never get any work done, what with customers wanting to talk to them all the time.

That, so Dave discovered, really wasn't a problem in leafy, authoritarian Guildford.

'Guildford could be a very strange place to live,' he confides. 'In the stockbroker belt, people are extremely private. It's all very money-orientated. They're not really concerned about you or who you are, so I was hardly recognised while I was working. It would probably be different nowadays because football is so much more fashionable than it was in the 1970s. But, back then, I was left alone to focus on the job in hand, which suited me, even though I'm naturally a very sociable person.'

Dave proved to be extremely adept at his new profession, which, given the uncanny similarities that exist between interior decorating and goalkeeping (yes, really!), probably shouldn't come as a great surprise.

'There is,' he points out, 'a discipline and a concentration to interior decorating. When I played in goal it was all about the penalty spot, the near post and the far post. They were the principal factors when it came to getting your bearings and angles right. The same thing applies to interior decorating. You've got to know where you are all of the time and really concentrate on what it is you're doing.'

Even so, a couple of chance encounters that occurred not long after he'd retired from professional football make you wonder whether Dave did in fact miss out on his true vocation in life.

'When I was about 12 or 13, I had a paper round that included delivering to Mr and Mrs Hollins, Dave's parents,' says Trevor Porter. 'This would have been when Dave and his family were living there while they were having their own house built. I knew all about Dave because I loved football, loved goalkeeping and I'd read up about him. It was actually my dad who went round on my behalf and asked if Dave could perhaps give me a few tips. That turned into us meeting every Sunday morning at 10am for practice sessions either at the local recreation ground or on this piece of common land. I couldn't believe it – I was one of the very few goalkeepers at that time, even among professionals, who had a coach. That lasted from when I was 13 through to when I signed apprentice forms at Fulham as a 15-year-old, right the way up until I turned pro with them at 17.'

Trevor spent two seasons at Fulham before going on to enjoy many more years as a goalkeeper with Slough Town and Brentford, alternating between a professional and semi-professional existence to accommodate his mushrooming window cleaning business (which, being the 1970s, earned him more dough than the football did).

'I learned so much from him football-wise but also in terms of being a man,' adds Trevor. 'Dave had a huge influence on me and still does to this day. And I've got to tell you this, he never took a penny off me or my dad for all the time he gave. Just think about that – a top-class Welsh international goalkeeper, albeit at the end of his career, giving me the time of day. I've got so much in life to thank him for.'

As indeed has Andrew Wycichowski, better known as 'Wishy' to his friends.

'Dave came down and did a bit of coaching at Milford Football Club in Guildford in the 1970s, which was where I was playing at the time,' says Andrew. 'My parents had split up and I'd spent time living between my grandparents and my mother, who'd met someone else. I saw things happening between my mother and father that nobody should see and I didn't get on with my stepfather either. I'd lost the plot, to be honest. I was an extremely angry young man who was having a terrible time and would take everything out on people through my football – getting booked, getting sent off, having a go at my team-mates to the point where they didn't want me in the team anymore. I wasn't the most pleasant of people. Then Dave started coming down and helping out. I was in awe of him, being this ex-professional football player. He had a lovely manner about him ... and he cared. I'd never had that at home. He not only became a steadying influence on me but also my inspiration.'

Over the years that followed, Andrew gradually conquered his demons and, with Dave's help, took his Level 2 coaching badge accredited by the Football Association. He went on to work at soccer camps in the USA, opened his own coaching school in the UK, oversaw the girls' football team at Charterhouse School in Surrey and became a deputy housemaster (as well as a football coach) at King Edward's Witley, an independent school also located in Surrey. He even briefly dated Dave's eldest daughter many, many moons ago.

'If it hadn't been for Dave, I wouldn't be where I am today,' declares Andrew. 'I would have gone the other way. There was a period of time where I was heavily into drink and some drugs. Dave helped steer me away from that and, later on, gave me a focal point when I decided I wanted to do my coaching certificates. He got in touch with his brother, John, who invited us along to Chelsea's training ground. I ended up going there for three days, just about scraped through my Level 2 coaching badge, got invited out to the USA and then rode this tidal wave of opportunity which came my way. Dave was the springboard to all that. I can't thank the man enough.'

He'd been a mentor to Andrew. He'd been a mentor to Trevor. He'd unwittingly acted as a mentor to many fledgling professionals at Newcastle United, several of whom had gone on to enjoy hugely successful careers at St James' Park and beyond. Didn't it ever cross Dave's mind that, perhaps, his future belonged in nurturing young talent, not interior decorating?

'No, for the simple reason that I had to concentrate on making a living,' he says, without any hint of regret. 'In those days football wages bought you a kind of semi-middle-class existence but, once you'd retired, they didn't continue to pay the bills, not unless you went on to become a top manager or coach. I had a family and I wanted to give them not only the best life but the best start in life. I couldn't do that by continuing in football. I'd had a wonderful upbringing with wonderful parents who guided me well, so when I saw someone who perhaps needed a leg-up then, yes, I wanted to help.

'Andrew, in particular, had a very difficult upbringing but I could see something in him. I could see he was a leader and I was proved to be right. I'm so proud of what he's done. The same applies to Trevor, who was one of seven children. I remember looking down at him from one of the upstairs windows as he delivered newspapers to my parents' house … and I saw myself looking back up. I could see me as a boy. I thought, *Yeah, I'll give him a couple of hours on a Sunday morning.* That Sunday morning lasted several years because he had real talent. I was never a believer in the mainstream coaching system anyway. To me, it seemed to be as much about making people conform as encouraging individuality. I simply wouldn't have been able to toe the line without getting frustrated. By doing my day job and helping people like Andrew and Trevor, I got to experience the best of both worlds.'

* * *

In 2018, a survey conducted by the Professional Players' Federation – an organisation dedicated to promoting, protecting and developing the interests of career sportsmen and women in the UK – found more than half of former professional sportspeople had experienced concerns about their mental and/or emotional well-being since retiring. Many of the survey's 800 respondents related struggling to find a sense of purpose having finished their careers, something that had on occasion opened the door to more serious problems such as depression, self-harm, addiction and financial problems. Others compared retirement to a grieving process.

'The biggest thing I felt was a loss of identity and purpose,' said double Olympic champion Kelly Holmes, who herself experienced post-career depression. 'Suddenly the structure, the people you call on, it all goes.'

In the 1960s and 1970s, such feelings and emotions existed among retired footballers but were, needless to say, barely discussed, certainly not in public. Stiff upper lip and all that. Lest it be forgotten, this was the generation that witnessed terrible things growing up during the Second World War. Everything is relative but, if you'd seen some of the things they had as children, there's always going to be a huge chunk of you that's glad just to be alive. Many ex-professional footballers, Eric and Dave included, had also played at a time when restrictive contracts meant they had few, if any, rights. With little or no job security, retirement wasn't some far-off spectre but an ever-present danger you had to learn to live with.

As far as Eric was concerned it wasn't the highs of winning that he missed, or the dressing room camaraderie, or the adulation of the fans, or the physical stimulation that comes with playing football. He'd been planning for his retirement since the day he became a hotelier. He already had a reason to get up every morning. What he did miss though was the competition ... which is where bowls came in.

'I didn't take up any other sport when I stopped playing football because I didn't really feel that I had the time,' says Eric. 'It was all hands on deck with the hotel. But I'm a competitive person, so there was a bit of a hole there. At one point a friend of mine said, "Why don't you come and play bowls?" And I said, "I don't want to play bowls. That's for old men!" Anyway, he managed to twist my arm and I've enjoyed every single minute of it ever since. I didn't want to start but, once I did, I thought, *I could be reasonably good at this*, because I seemed to get the hang of it straightaway. And I've had some good times. I've had my moments.'

That he has. In fact, Eric even got to play for the Sussex county side during the 1990s.

'It's funny, isn't it?' he adds. 'I never won a cap for playing football but I did for playing bowls! That was nice.

It was all very understated, as bowls tends to be. I got a phone call and they said, "Look, we've got a team, there's a match against such-and-such a county, we want you to play. Would you be alright with that?" And I said, "Sure. Of course." It was an honour, to be fair, something I really didn't expect.'

So, Eric, given the reputation bowls has as a somewhat sedentary sport for 'old men', go ahead, sell it to us …

'First of all it's great company because there's a lot of you playing. You get with your mates, you play your game, you have your cup of tea afterwards. It's all very enjoyable. And it's not just for men – it's open to all people of all ages. Of course, when you start, you're only playing for fun. You're learning the ropes. Then, when you get to like it, you start to get serious. You'll want to play in the league and the cup games. In that respect it's no different to playing football or any other sport – the more you play, the more you want to play, and the more competitive it gets. And, hopefully, the more you play, the better you'll get. Try it. You might not think you'll like it, but I bet you do.'

It took Dave a little while longer to discover the hidden pleasures of bowls. Quite why Eric didn't try to convert him beforehand, he's not entirely sure. Then again, as Eric says, 'Bowls has a habit of finding you when you're ready for it.'

'After I finished playing football, I was approached by the father of someone I knew who asked me if I would be interested in becoming a Freemason,' Dave recalls. 'I didn't have much of a social life at that point so I thought, *That's not a bad idea*. It's a men-only thing, which was something I was used to, having been in football my whole life. I did that for a few years, meeting all sorts of people like John Sainsbury, the businessman, and the old kipper tie comedian Arthur English. I know it's seen as this secret society with funny connotations but I quite enjoyed it. The downside was you're out all the time, which meant I wasn't seeing enough of Jackie.

'My older brother, Roy, had become pretty good at bowls and was playing for Surrey. It was him who said, "Why don't you come down and give it a go?" It struck me that bowls was something Jackie and I could perhaps do together. So I packed in the Freemasons and booked us both six lessons. After the first one the coach said to me, "David, you're going to need all your lessons because your fingers are smashed up and there's a lot of technique to work on. But your wife doesn't need any more." I said, "Why's that?" And he said, "Because she's a complete natural." It turned out Jackie had what it took right from the start.'

And so Dave and Jackie started playing every week at the Wey Valley Indoor Bowls Club in Guildford, he as a keen amateur, she as a rising star who went on to represent Surrey at the All England Open Championships. Meanwhile, down in Sussex, Eric and Ida were tearing up the rinks together in their spare time at Denton Island Bowls Club, situated just along the south coast from Brighton in the town of Newhaven. Every so often the fixture schedule would pair the two clubs against each other. Sadly, especially as Eric and Dave never got to be on opposing teams as footballers, the stars never quite aligned when it came to bowling either. There are weekday leagues and weekend friendlies and morning games and afternoon games and cup games and games for different abilities and all sorts. It's the Clapham Junction of British sport, is bowls, and unfortunately Eric and Dave's trains ran on different tracks at different times.

Mind you, given their competitive natures, perhaps that's not necessarily a bad thing.

'It's always about competing, no matter who you're up against,' maintains Dave.

'Always got to win, me,' adds Eric. 'Always.'

'What makes the difference between a game and a sport?' asks actor Vince Vaughn, rhetorically, in the 2003 comedy film *Blackball*, based around bowls, before answering in a single word – 'Passion!' True, bowls can't hold a candle to association football in the passion stakes. Folk don't travel in their thousands to watch it and, once there, sing, shout, swear or cry during matches. We're most certainly not talking about 'a force that mobilises the sentiments of a people in a way that nothing else can', as Nelson Mandela described football.

There is, nonetheless, a steely competitiveness to bowls that underpins its whole existence. Yes, it's sociable. Yes, it's enjoyable. Yes, there's a cup of tea (and a slice of cake, if you're lucky) waiting for you afterwards. But don't be fooled by its cosy exterior. Underneath, bowls is deadly serious, which might explain why so many refugees from other more physical sports – football, hockey, netball, rugby – defect to it in later life for their competitive fix.

'It is a very good leisurely activity,' says Dave. 'I've made more friends playing bowls than I ever did as a professional footballer, probably because the environment is more relaxed and you're in people's company all the time. It's not like being a goalkeeper, when you're out there all alone on the field. But it is a highly skilful game, one women take to just as easily as men. I mean my wife was deadly. If you're going to play at a decent level, then you've got to be good. It's not just a question of picking up a bowl and bowling it. It's knowing exactly what you have to do with it. In that department it doesn't matter whether you're 9 or 90 – if you've got it, then you've got it. Age is irrelevant.'

They say that sport and physical activity is good for the body – your bones, your heart, your weight, etc. They say sport can tackle inequalities in society. They say sport and exercise counters loneliness. They say exercise can reduce the risk and even slow the progression of dementia. They are, in the main, right about all these things and more, which is good news for Eric and Dave and everyone else who plays bowls or partakes in any sport or type of exercise.

Yet, as anyone who follows the news on a regular basis will be aware, they may also – at least when it comes to football – be wrong.

12

SHAMEFUL

'People in football will look after you when it's in their interests to look after you. When it's not in their interests, they won't.' – Jack Charlton

ROD TAYLOR was 72 years old when, in 2016, he stopped wanting to attend football matches at Fratton Park. In the years immediately prior to that the former Portsmouth, Gillingham and Bournemouth midfielder – a 'wing-half', as it was in his day – had seen his health gradually decline to the point where he was becoming increasingly housebound. His family noticed subtle behavioural changes in 2008, although it wasn't for another two years that the first truly alarming incident – becoming confused, disorientated and ultimately lost while attempting to take a lift instead of climbing some stairs – occurred. Unable to reverse his car out of a driveway, he stopped driving altogether. Then there were the falls, night and day, not to mention the hallucinations. In March 2018, Rod was admitted to respite care but within days had been hospitalised with a broken hip following another fall. No longer able to speak or swallow and having developed pneumonia and sepsis, he died the following month. 'When things were getting bad he would point at his head with his two fingers as if to imitate a gun,' Rod's daughter Rachel told the *Daily Telegraph* in August that year. 'He was 74 but looked like he was 94.'

Keith Pontin from Pontyclun in South Wales played for Cardiff City between 1976 and 1983 and had, like Dave Hollins, been decorated with full Wales honours. In 2015, following concerns about his mental decline, he was diagnosed with dementia at the age of 59. He died five years later. Keith was, in the words of his widow Janet, a 'great husband, a great dad, a great laugh', whose condition, so she believed, was caused by years of heading footballs coupled with multiple concussions. Coroner David Regan agreed with her. At the inquest into Pontin's death, Regan said, 'It seems to me on the balance of probabilities, having found Keith had repeated head contact with the ball, I'm driven to the conclusion it more than minimally, negligibly, or trivially contributed to his death. I have no evidence that he suffered head trauma at any other stage in his life.'

Gordon Nutt was 76 years old when, in 2008, he made his last visit to the UK from his adopted Australia. Back in the day, Gordon, a skilful right-winger, had entertained the crowds at numerous clubs, including Coventry City, Cardiff City and Arsenal, turning out 51 times for the Gunners (including the last match played by Manchester United on English soil prior to the Munich air disaster, a wildly entertaining spectacle at Highbury that Arsenal lost 5-4). Now, as his memory ebbed away, Gordon was visiting his old haunts before they ceased meaning anything to him. With wife Jennifer at his side, he walked the streets of north London. He walked the streets of Coventry. He walked the streets of Cardiff where, one afternoon, spotting a small boy kicking a ball around in a park, he made a beeline to join in (that small boy just happened to be your author's then two-year-old son). The trip, so Jennifer recalled in 2011 (by which time Gordon required round-the-clock care, paid for largely by the Australian federal government, thereby enabling him to stay at home), had been a 'cathartic' experience at an increasingly difficult time for the both of them. By the time he died in March 2014, Gordon had no idea what a football even was.

It was in 2002, following the death of the former West Bromwich Albion and England centre-forward Jeff Astle, that researchers first began to take a serious look at the potential link between football and dementia. Initially, it was believed Astle had died from Alzheimer's disease. However, the coroner at his inquest ruled that his brain had in fact been damaged by heading footballs, as in the heavy leather ones prevalent during his playing days.

In 2014, the eminent neuropathologist Dr Willie Stewart carried out a fresh examination of Astle's brain and found that he had been suffering from what is known as chronic traumatic encephalopathy (CTE), a specific type of dementia and neurological disease triggered by repetitive head trauma. CTE is progressive and typically affects a person's behaviour, memory and ability to think. It can only be diagnosed for certain at a post-mortem. Once upon a time, CTE was more commonly referred to as 'punch-drunk syndrome' and associated with boxing, along more recently with American football. Although many footballers in Britain had died after suffering from dementia, their brains were never examined, meaning a link to CTE couldn't be confirmed. Jeff Astle's was the first brain to be examined. Rod Taylor's was the second.

Since Dr Stewart carried out that fresh examination of Astle's brain, so the list of famous footballing names either dying with, suffering from or being treated for Alzheimer's and/or dementia has mounted – Jack Charlton, Bobby Charlton, Nobby Stiles, Martin Peters, Ray Wilson, Gordon McQueen, Frank Worthington, Denis Law, Gordon Cowans, Dave Watson, Terry McDermott, Chris Nicholl. Then there are the countless others you don't get to hear about because they're not as famous or are suffering in silence, either at their own behest or that of their family. It's a tragedy on a monumental scale, one football's authorities as of yet appear shamefully reluctant to tackle full on.

'Every slice of my dad's brain had trauma in it,' Dawn Astle, Jeff's daughter, said in March 2021. 'We assumed incorrectly that the inquest ruling of industrial disease would be a defining moment. In any other industry a finding like that would have earthquake-like repercussions. Not football. My dad's death didn't matter. I believe football's privileged status of self-governing is why. They should hang their heads in shame.'

'It was something I was totally unaware of until it started appearing in the papers,' says Eric. 'I never realised it was happening. It was certainly never spoken about when I was a player. But, then again, we were young at the time. It's only when you're older that it catches up with you. We used to head these big leather balls with big laces in matches and in training. Well, I say we – I didn't, and neither did Dave, because we were goalkeepers. It was our defenders who did all the heading along with the centre-forwards up the other end. The only heading I'd do was head tennis in training, which I loved. You know, string up a net and have five-a-sides heading the ball backwards and forwards over it. I don't suppose they'd do that now, not if they are trying to reduce the amount of heading they're doing.'

'Jeff Astle changed everything, not that he knew it, poor soul,' adds Dave. 'That's when I became aware of it. They – and I mean outfield players – just headed it, because that was their occupation. I never heard of anybody discussing the weight of the ball, or the ball itself, or what it might do to you. Looking back, I do recall a centre-half who used to play for Newcastle United – Bill Thompson was his name – who came from near Ashington, where the Charlton brothers were from. He died of dementia. I remember speaking to his wife and, from what she said, I think that was probably down to him heading the ball all the time. So you make the connections … but only now. Then, not so.'

Given their ages, you could argue Eric and Dave remained oblivious to the issue until relatively recently because, well, all bar a couple of their former team-mates are now dead. Dementia in football only came to light in the 21st century. A fair percentage of Eric and Dave's cohort never even got to see the year 2000. Those of a slightly younger vintage, however, seemed to have cottoned on much earlier.

'I can remember going to an Albion celebratory do to mark an anniversary of when we'd won the old Fourth Division in 1965,' recalls Brian Powney, who played 386 times in goal for Brighton & Hove Albion between 1962 and 1974. 'Sitting on the same table as me that evening were two of my old team-mates who I could see both had a problem. A few years previously I'd been on a break in a part of England where one of them lived and, quite by chance, I'd bumped into him. There I was, sitting by the marina having a coffee, and he walked by. I wasn't sure it was him at first, so I followed him down the road until he stopped to look in a shop window, at which point he turned and saw me – "****ing hell, it's Joe Powney!" he said, because everyone at Brighton used to call me Joe. When we were at that reunion, I reminded him of how we'd met that day ... and he was totally blank. Couldn't remember it at all. And this had only been five years or so beforehand. Needless to say, several other members of that team have now either passed away through dementia or are suffering from it. It's a terrible thing, it really is.'

Between them, Eric Gill, Dave Hollins, Charlie Baker (who took over in Brighton's goal from Dave) and Brian Powney (who subsequently took over from Charlie) have a combined age somewhere in the mid-300s. All four are not only still with us but have excellent recall. All four played in the one position on the football field where you rarely head the ball. Coincidence? Maybe, maybe not. All four of them did suffer concussions, so it's not as if they came away unscathed from the neck up.

Then again, research by Dr Stewart has revealed that, besides being four times more likely to suffer from

Alzheimer's and other neurodegenerative diseases than the general public, footballers are more at risk according to the position they played in. For defenders, the increased risk is fivefold. For forwards, it's threefold. Goalkeepers, on the other hand, were found to have no increased risk when compared to the general population.

'A few years ago I was asked by the Professional Footballers' Association if I'd go up to Loughborough University to take part in a study into Alzheimer's and dementia through the heading of footballs,' adds Brian Powney. 'They wanted me to be examined and talk to them about my experiences, but I said, "Look, I was a goalkeeper, I didn't head the ball." Well, not intentionally anyway. So I didn't do it because they never came back to me after that. Part of me wonders whether I should have gone because there's only one way they can compare the risks from position to position and that's by examining players from right across the field, including goalkeepers. I did get laid out twice in my career, after all, as in concussed. On both occasions I wasn't able to remember a thing afterwards. But, as I said, they never got back to me.'

Dave has another theory, or rather a hunch, regarding football and dementia, which despite being scientifically unproven makes for interesting hearing.

'Although the link to heading the ball is undeniable, I started wondering whether there was in fact something else to it, because not everyone who has suffered played in a position where they headed the ball,' he says. 'Take, for instance, Peter Bonetti, the Chelsea and England goalkeeper, who suffered with dementia throughout the last few years of his life. He was a great friend of my brother John. After Peter died, John said to me, "How could Peter have got dementia if he wasn't heading the ball?" That got me wondering whether it might be something to do with nervous tension. When you go out to play in front of thousands and thousands of people, your nerves are really taut. Different players have different ways of dealing with that. Some are physically sick beforehand. Some used to have a crafty cigarette in the toilets. Some had a swig of whisky or brandy. They did whatever they had to do to get themselves out of the dressing room, on to the pitch and into the game. But none of that changed the fact that every week their nerves were taut, to the point of going haywire.'

Which is something, presumably, Dave would like to see research being carried out on, providing it hasn't already?

'I would, yes, because I don't think it has been looked into. You see, it's very easy to say it's all about the ball impacting the head. John and I were thinking along exactly the same lines after Peter died and I don't think we're the only ones who reckon there might be something in this. Imagine you're about to play in the Maracanã Stadium, like we did, against Brazil. There are 100,000 or 200,000 people out there. You start off in the dressing room below ground. You come out and start to climb the steps up towards the pitch. All of a sudden, it hits you … this noise. It's incredible. And the adrenalin is going. Your heart is pumping. The tension inside your body, which has been building ever since you woke up that morning, is immense. Some people thrive on that kind of atmosphere while others dread it, but regardless of how you feel every player experiences it. Whether that's good for the human body, on a regular basis over the course of many years, I just don't know. None of us do.'

'I'm still here but it has made me wonder how many of the boys I played with over all those years suffered with it,' says Eric. 'You tend to go in different directions when you stop playing, so there's no way of knowing how many of them stopped living before their time.'

Except that sometimes there is. The stigma associated with Alzheimer's and dementia, especially among the older strata of society, means it's a subject that's difficult to talk about for many, especially on the record and in public. During the writing of this book, the wife of one former Brighton & Hove Albion player – still alive, but suffering from advanced dementia – offered up a heart-wrenching glimpse into how dementia has burned its way through one particular group of former players.

'The wives know the true extent of it because we're the ones left behind,' she said while studying a black-and-white team photograph showing her husband standing alongside several faces familiar to Eric and Dave. 'He's not here anymore, he's not here anymore, he's not here anymore, I don't know about him, he's not here anymore, he's still alive, he's not here anymore, he's not here anymore, he's not here anymore, he's not here anymore, he's still alive, I'm not sure about him, he's not here anymore, and he's not here anymore. Of those, I'd say four or maybe five suffered with dementia. That's just one team that played for one club at one particular time. Multiply that by all the clubs in the country, if not the world ... well, it doesn't bear thinking about.'

'If you're going to play in a game of football and you're not a goalkeeper, then you're going to have to head the ball at some time or other,' declares Eric. 'You can't stop that unless you change the way the whole game is played. The only thing now I suppose is that the ball is much lighter than it once was. There are no laces in it. It doesn't get heavier when it gets wet. The balls of today are not like those medicine balls we used when I played. Surely that's got to be a good thing?'

You'd think so, wouldn't you? However, further research by Dr Stewart has shown that players today are potentially at greater risk not only as they tend to head the ball more often, but because modern lighter balls travel faster, thereby resulting in a greater impact.

'The slightly heavier leather balls travelled through the air slower than the lighter ones, so the risk impact forces are transmitted more by the speed than the weight of the ball,' Dr Stewart commented in August 2021. 'So, with the faster modern balls, and more heading in the modern game than 50 years ago, so potentially the [dementia] risk could be greater. There's no evidence that anything that has changed in the game up to the 1990s has changed risk. To know that we would need to wait another 20 years at least. And that's too long.'

'I've thought for a long time that there was something wrong with the modern ball,' says Dave. 'When I first started out you had the old leather footballs, the medicine balls, with the laces. Then along came the Mitre ball, which I loved playing with. You always knew exactly where you were with the Mitre ball in terms of its design and the way it moved through the air. With the modern-day ball, how many times do you see a forward or a defender go to head it and the ball will fly off, at pace, way past the target or at a completely different angle to how you expected it to travel?

'It's the same with goalkeepers. How many times do you see somebody hit a dead ball from 30 yards out and it goes in without the goalkeeper seeming to move? I used to think, *What the hell's happened there?* Then I worked it out. It's because the ball has moved in an unnatural way in the air. Sometimes a goalkeeper will just punch a ball that's coming straight at them back out into play instead of catching it. Again, that's because it has moved unnaturally – best just to fist it away rather than try and catch it and be made to look a fool. Except that fisting it away means you're putting the ball straight back out into the danger area! Instead of improving the game, the modern ball is in danger of destroying it. I mean that in terms of being a spectacle as well as any potential wider health issues. These are things that need to be thoroughly discussed.'

* * *

'He who rejects change is the architect of decay.' So said the former Labour Prime Minister Harold Wilson, who was himself rejected by the British electorate just a matter of months before Aldershot, and the world of professional football in general, rejected Dave. Given that the older we get, the more resistant to change we supposedly become, you might expect our two ex-goalkeepers to be fully paid-up members of the Grouchy Club at this late stage of their lives, especially when it comes to football matters and in light of Dave's despair at the modern ball. You would, in the main, be wrong.

'I think football, like most things in this world, has progressed and got better,' says Eric. 'I reckon the teams of today could beat the teams of yesterday. The way footballers are looked after, the way they eat, the way they train, it's all improved. They are no longer slaves like we were – that had to change. They no longer play ankle-deep in mud and puddles but get to stroke the ball around so it goes exactly where they want it to go. The goalkeepers get more protection. And look at the gloves they wear now! No more of those old string ones that we had to use. Mind you, they were better than the alternatives, which was to play in your bare hands or wear woollen or leather ones. At least the string ones were a bit bobbly, which meant you could get a better grip.'

'Oh my Lord, string gloves,' adds Dave, laughing. 'Now, this is what I used to do. I'd go to a local tailor's and buy my own pairs of string gloves. Then I'd cut out the insides, which consisted of wool, and leave it so you had nothing left but the string itself. That would allow the gloves to dry out during games because your body would be getting hotter and hotter as the match wore on. That was my theory anyway. It must have worked because you could hold on to the ball quite easily with them in slippery conditions.'

However, association football has a nasty habit of resisting or embracing change when it's most or least needed respectively. Take the unfolding dementia crisis, for example. Or the catalogue of disasters at matches throughout the 1970s and 1980s, which the game's authorities failed to properly address until political and judicial pressure, combined with falling attendances at matches, forced them into doing so. It's here where Dave is by far and away the more vociferous of the two men.

'Football is quick to move when there's a European Super League to discuss or sponsorship deals to be struck or any kind of money to be made,' he says. 'When it comes to more serious matters, such as the well-being of the fans, it's almost nowhere to be seen. Not long after I retired professionally, the Ibrox Stadium disaster occurred up in Scotland when over 60 people were crushed to death at a Celtic versus Rangers game through no fault of their own. You had the start of all the terrace violence between fans as football became more tribal. You had the Bradford fire [in 1985] where a similar number of people perished as at Ibrox, again through no fault of their own. You had the Heysel Stadium disaster [also in 1985] when all those poor Juventus supporters died at the European Cup Final. You had the Hillsborough disaster [in 1989] at the Liverpool versus Nottingham Forest FA Cup semi-final and the cover-up afterwards into what actually happened that day.

'You had all these events and more, year after year, and yet nothing was ever done. Until, that is, after Hillsborough, when stadiums became all-seater. Ever since then it has become more and more expensive to go and watch football. Something that was done in the name of safety became, to all intents and purposes, a money-making exercise. The ordinary bloke in the street can't afford to go anymore. What was a working-class sport has become a middle-class sport. The modern game has lost its human touch.'

And don't get him started on video technology:

'VAR [the video assistant referee, a match official who reviews decisions made by the referee on the field while a match is in progress] drives me mad. Football is all about movement. If you're stopping that movement on a regular basis, sometimes for two or three minutes at a time, to try and establish something so borderline that it's still dividing opinion after umpteen replays, then football stops being football as we know it. It's certainly not entertainment.'

... or current coaching trends involving the role of goalkeepers:

'It's getting to the point where the position is being totally nullified, bordering on obsolete. They're not goalkeepers anymore – they're sweepers, kind of in the same vein as ice hockey goaltenders. They play more with their feet than their hands. That's not goalkeeping. It's almost as if they're not allowed to use their initiative anymore, like on goal kicks when they have to play the ball short to a defender who's standing right beside them. If you don't restart play that way, then you get dropped by the manager. Because goalkeepers are playing more like sweepers and handling the ball less, we're at the stage where they're getting caught off their line or not coming for balls inside their six-yard box that they really should be coming for. Jackie can't bear to be in the same room as me if I'm watching football on television. It annoys me *that* much.'

On the other hand, Dave is thrilled that players now benefit from the very best medical expertise both on and off the pitch ('instead of being butchered by well-meaning amateurs') and doesn't begrudge them the wages they receive either ('the natural reaction to the abolition of the maximum wage and the fact we were treated like slaves – they're getting what we didn't get').

As for the increased participation of women right the way across the sport? Dave's all for it, as befits a man with two daughters whose wife played competitive netball and bowls.

'I was watching television one evening and there were two people, a man and a woman, discussing a Premier League game,' he says. 'The guy was someone who had played professionally. And I actually felt the woman was doing a far better job of analysing it than him. She talked so much sense, tactically as well as in general. The words coming out of her mouth were just right. I don't think it matters who is commentating or doing the post-match analysis, so long as they are making sense and doing a good job of it. And if that commentary or analysis is coming to you from a Women's Super League match, then even better! Football, after all, is supposed to be the people's game. That should mean all people.'

Over the course of their football careers, Eric and Dave were kicked, barged, punched, kneed and stamped on routinely by opponents. They suffered concussions and, in Dave's case, spells in hospital. To a degree, both men saw their top-line Football League days ended prematurely by the drip-drip effect of injuries and attrition. And yet, compared to so many of their contemporaries, they appear to have come through relatively unscathed. Neither of them are quite sure how.

'On paper, it's a safer game now, and that can only be a good thing,' says Eric, who takes a smorgasbord of tablets these days to boost his iron, thin his blood and counter atrial fibrillation (an irregular, often very rapid heart rhythm). 'This dementia business is terrible though, absolutely terrible. I guess I dodged a bullet there, you could say, being a goalkeeper. If it was going to happen to me then I reckon it would have happened by now. Touch wood, I'm feeling good. I walk every day and do what exercise I can. You've got to keep going or you'll seize up!'

As for Dave?

'I take blood pressure pills and a steroid-based nasal drop to help with the linings of my nostrils, which I destroyed by taking Vicks before games.'

Say what?

'It's a ritual I used to go through about half an hour before kick-off. I'd put some Vicks up one nostril, then some Vicks up the other nostril, and I found that soothed any nerves and helped me focus on the match in hand. Then I'd repeat it again at half-time. The problem was, after I retired, I discovered that little ritual had destroyed 80 per cent of the lining in my nose and caused polyps to grow in the nasal passages, which had to be removed. Eventually it all settled down with the help of steroids. Now I take a steroid-based nasal drop once a day, just before I go to bed. I turn my head around so it's at a funny angle and I drop it in. It's as I said – some players used to be sick before matches, some would have a cigarette in the toilets, some would have a swig of something strong like whisky, and I would put

Vicks up my nose. And, in the long run, it didn't do me any good! But I'm not complaining. Compared to what some former players like Jeff Astle had to go through, that's a small price to pay.'

13

AUTUMN

'Any football club, any person, any human being alive goes through adversity. The art of living life is to recover from that and to respond to any challenges being thrown at you.' –
Peter Schmeichel

RUNNING A hotel, as anyone who has ever tried it will tell you, is hard work. There are guests to check in and guests to check out and rooms to clean and mouths to feed and maintenance to be done and drinks to be served and telephones to be answered and suppliers to be paid and queries to be dealt with and staff to be looked after and inspectors to think about and health and safety to adhere to. And it *never* stops – 4pm or 4am, you're always on call.

It's even harder when someone is trying to blow the place up.

As a popular tourist destination and the host of many a political event, Brighton was always a potential target during the 1970s, 1980s and 1990s for the Provisional Irish Republican Army. From 1969 until 1998, Northern

Ireland appeared to come apart at the seams as Catholics (generally supporting the reunification of Ireland) and Protestants (insistent on remaining part of Britain) clashed in what became known as 'the Troubles'. Thousands died and thousands more were injured.

For those living in Northern Ireland, the bombings and revenge killings weren't far short of a daily occurrence. The danger was certainly ever-present as indeed it sometimes felt in England, especially London. That's because every so often it wasn't Belfast, Derry or Lisburn that were in the news but settlements on the mainland, such as Birmingham, Manchester and even Guildford, where, on the evening of 5 October 1974, the IRA detonated bombs in two pubs – The Horse and Groom and The Seven Stars – popular with British Army personnel stationed at the nearby Pirbright barracks, killing five people and injuring another 65.

One day in September 1984, a man by the name of Patrick Magee checked into The Grand Hotel in Brighton, just a short walk along the seafront from Eric and Ida Gill's establishment, under the pseudonym Roy Walsh. During his stay Magee planted a bomb with a long delay timer under the bath in his room on the sixth floor. A little over three weeks later, at approximately 2.54am on 12 October, the bomb exploded on the eve of the last day of the Conservative Party conference, causing a five-ton chimney stack to crash through the hotel. Five people were killed and dozens more injured (the casualty list would, in all likelihood, have been far higher had it not been for the hotel's sturdy Victorian design). Prime Minister Margaret Thatcher, the IRA's principal target, escaped unharmed despite her suite being damaged. It later emerged that Magee had visited Brighton as far back as 1977 to case senior figures in the then Labour Party government as potential targets.

'Mrs Thatcher will now realise that Britain can't occupy our country and torture our prisoners and shoot our people in their own streets and get away with it,' declared the IRA in claiming responsibility for the bombing (Thatcher's unbending stance during the 1981 hunger strikes by Irish republican prisoners had made her a hate figure in nationalist circles). 'Today we were unlucky, but remember we only have to be lucky once. You will have to be lucky always. Give Ireland peace and there will be no more war.'

The attack on The Grand Hotel, one of the town's most iconic buildings, left a pall over Brighton mentally as well as physically. For all the layers of security that accompanied any visit by a senior politician, the IRA had still managed to find a way through. And, as the mainland targets became more random – railway stations, litter bins, office blocks, etc, rather than places frequented by more obvious marks such as politicians and the military – so the sense of unease, rather than outright fear, intensified. They'd done it once – why wouldn't they try again? After all, in the IRA's eyes they had been 'unlucky' first time around.

'I can't remember how it was that I heard the news about The Grand but, as soon as I did, I pulled my clothes on and walked straight down there,' recalls Eric. 'I'll never forget the sight that greeted me as I stood by the sea looking up at it. There were police everywhere and this great big gap down the middle of the hotel like a giant scar.

I thought, *Blimey, if they're going to start blowing up hotels, I hope they ain't going to blow up mine!* Seriously though, it did make me worry a bit. You think, *They've blown up The Grand! What's stopping them going for somewhere else?* You never know what's in the minds of people who are prepared to do something like that. I can't remember if it was around that time – it may well have been – but this guy turned up at our hotel one day who our dog, Skipper, a golden Labrador, took an instant dislike to. I had 14 wonderful years with Skipper and he was the most laid-back dog you could ever wish to meet, but he took one look at this guy and started growling at him. He knew this guy was no good and stood his ground. It was really, really strange. Eventually the guy turned around and left. That did make me think. I mean, if anything's going to sniff out a bomb, then it's going to be a dog.'

A little over a year later, in December 1985, Eric handed over the keys to Simpson's. What happened at The Grand Hotel had, he maintains, no bearing on his decision. He was simply made an offer neither he, nor Ida, could refuse.

'I'd had a good run by that time and I got good money for it, so there were no regrets, none whatsoever,' says Eric. 'A friend of mine introduced me to a young lady who advised me how best to invest the money I got for it. And she advised me well because I haven't had to work since! I'm still drawing that to this day. But I earned it alright. If you want an easy life, don't run a hotel. It's tough and the hours are all hours – but I'm glad I did it.'

Bowls. Walks along the chalk hills of the North Downs. Walks along the chalk hills of the South Downs.

Watching their children grow up. Becoming grandparents. Enjoying the fruits of their second careers before retiring all over again. These, to paraphrase Frank Sinatra, were very good years for Eric and Dave who, with time on their hands and the latter having scratched his north of England itch, were now seeing more of each other than at any point since their playing days at Brighton & Hove Albion. Which kind of makes it sound as if football, the thing that initially brought them together, had taken a back seat.

'I suppose it did with me,' admits Eric. 'I still got recognised around town, which was nice. I had a cabinet made while we had the hotel which contained all my trophies and things. That became a bit of a talking point – "Oh, it's YOU! I didn't realise it was YOU! What did you do to get this one? What did you do to get that one?" It made a lot of our guests feel more at home because it was personal. You know, they could put a name to me and the place they'd come to spend some time. If you get your guests talking together about something like that, then it adds to the atmosphere. And if they weren't interested in football, then it didn't matter to me. There was a picture in there of me receiving my Army Cup medal from the King and the Queen Mother. People loved that. I had the medal beside it so they could see for themselves what I'd been presented with. But, once I sold the hotel, that all went into boxes. Of course, my son kept on playing football, so I still had that link for a while.'

'I did indeed,' says Steve Gill who, despite not making the grade at West Ham United, enjoyed a long semi-professional career with several non-league football clubs, including Hastings United and Worthing. 'I was very lucky to be at West Ham at that time, to get to see and train alongside all those stars week in, week out. I did four trips abroad with them, including one to Africa. But, in the end, I didn't quite make it. It was fun while it lasted, though, and it didn't stop there because I loved playing non-league. There are hundreds if not thousands of young players who give up the game altogether because they don't get to make it professionally. I didn't want that to be me.'

With Dave, things were slightly different. Given his family's close association with the game, it was perhaps always going to be so. Between 1975 and 1983, brother John clocked up almost 300 appearances for Queens Park Rangers and Arsenal combined before embarking on one last hurrah as a player back at Chelsea, the club where he'd made his professional debut in 1963. After hanging up his boots he went on to manage, you've guessed it, Chelsea, prior to taking the reins at Swansea City, Rochdale and Crawley Town, with a brief spell as caretaker boss at Queens Park Rangers thrown in. When Dave wasn't playing bowls, mentoring Trevor Porter or Andrew Wycichowski, helping out at Milford Football Club or attending the occasional player reunion in Newcastle, he could usually be found somewhere in the stands supporting his brother.

On the subject of John Hollins, here's a question for you that has been known to come up in the occasional pub quiz:

'Which two brothers, born and raised in Britain, played international football for different countries?'

Answer – Dave Hollins (Wales) and John Hollins (England).

The pleasure, as and when that gets asked and you triumph by a single point, is all ours. Quite why Dave wasn't at Wembley Stadium to witness John's only full England cap, a 2-0 win versus Spain in May 1967, he can't quite remember. Safe to say, it must have been something pretty damned important to thwart him.

Then there was the spaced-out encounter from more recent times, which veered more into the realms of a David Lynch movie than anything to do with football.

'I always used to get kidney stones and was forever going into hospital to get them removed,' says Dave. 'One day I was in the Surrey County Hospital in Guildford, sitting upright in bed with my nebuliser on. All of a sudden, I notice this kerfuffle just outside my room. Then the doors burst open and there's this entourage gathered around this chap who was being brought in. I'm lying there, watching all of this going on, looking at the chap who has been rushed in, and then it suddenly dawns on me – *that's Paul Gascoigne!*

'I suppose it must have been something to do with drink or drugs, or maybe his mental health, because the police were there as well. Once things had calmed down, I took out a pen and a piece of paper and wrote a note, which I passed to one of the nurses to give to him. "My name is Dave Hollins, brother of John Hollins, and I played for Newcastle from 1961 to 1967. I'm just across the way from you. How are you, Paul?" He was well out of it though, so I never received a reply. But at least I made the effort.'

* * *

In 2022, the average life expectancy of a person in the UK, according to the United Nations, was 81 (or 81.65, to be exact). In 1950, when Eric and Dave turned 20 and 12, respectively, it was 68 (or, for the benefit of any pedants out there, 68.69). Life expectancy statistics can and indeed do fluctuate according to various socio-economic factors such as where you live, how you live and whether you're male or female, but there we have the ballpark figures. Better than many countries (Argentina 77.03) yet worse than quite a few others (Spain 83.86). The good news, though, is that people in the UK, by and large, are now living longer. The flip side of the coin is that by living longer, they're likely to run into more health-related problems along the way.

Ida Gill was in her late seventies when the liver cancer that would eventually kill her first manifested itself. She saw a specialist in Guildford. She spent time in hospital in Brighton. The general consensus on all fronts was an operation would be too dangerous. Consequently, Ida made the best of what time on Earth she had left, including (being the meticulous soul she was) leaving written instructions to family members concerning where various important documents and mementoes were kept. She died at home on 9 November 2012, just a couple of months after her 80th birthday, with Eric and son Steve at her side. Peaceful, so it was, just as she'd wanted. Then again, don't we all?

Eric is a good talker, as you, dear reader, will probably have realised by now. It's here, however, even after several years, that the words dry up.

'He does find it difficult to talk about,' confides Steve. 'He adored mum and they were such young lovers. She was only 19 when she gave birth to me. All that time, you could tell how in love with each other they were. From a son's point of view, both my brother and I were so lucky to have such loving parents. They'd loved each other almost as long as they could remember, right the way back to when he would come out of his flat in Camden and take the long route to work on the off chance that he might catch a glimpse of her through the kitchen window of her flat. If she was there, then they'd wave to each other and he'd double-back on himself behind the flats and head off to work. Theirs was a proper love story.'

'I'm pretty sure it was Steve who'd phoned us in the days beforehand, so we kind of knew what to expect, not that it made it any easier,' says Dave. 'I'd known Ida my entire adult life, as had my wife, Jackie. She was a lovely woman, she really was. We came down from Guildford for the funeral and afterwards everyone went back to the bowls club at Denton Island, which seemed like the perfect venue. Invariably the women are nearly always better bowlers than the men, and that was certainly the case with Eric and me.'

At which point Dave, another rarely lost for words, runs out of words.

'It was a lovely funeral, it really was,' adds Jackie. 'You know how some funerals are a real celebration of life? Well Ida's certainly was, which is something she would have loved. It was a wonderful turnout, especially from the bowling fraternity, with many people wearing their bowling blazers. Eric and her made such a devoted couple.

It was always Eric and Ida, never one or the other. Always Eric *and* Ida. She'd been like a second mum to Dave back when we first met, and she always said he was like a third son. Which is funny, because there really wasn't much of an age gap between them! So, yes, it was incredibly sad, but it was also a fitting send-off.'

In the years since, Eric has found companionship as much as love with Irene Taylor, better known as 'Rene', somebody he'd already known for some considerable time who, needless to say, shares his passion for bowls.

'We'd been friends for 20 or more years because Ida and I often used to play bowls with Rene and Alan, her husband,' says Eric. 'Then Ida died and Alan also died, so we were left on our own. And it just went from there. We've never married – that's way too complicated, what with family and property and money. But we do live together and it's really, really good. I'd like to say we look after each other. She certainly looks after me. Every morning she puts my pills out – the ones I take for my heart, my iron and my digestion – and reminds me to take them. I take so many I rattle after I swallow them! To have someone by your side at this stage of life is wonderful.'

'I had to have a back operation in 2015, which meant no bowling for me for a while,' says Rene. 'While I was recuperating, he came round with a bunch of flowers, which I thought was a lovely thing to do. I said, "Thank you very much." He came in for a cup of tea and we just clicked. He's ever the gentleman with things like that, the kind of man who will open a car door for you. In fact, I had to say, "Please don't bring me any more flowers," because every time he came to visit, he'd have another bunch! To begin with he always used to go home but, what with me having had my operation, he ended up staying and looking after me. And, although he's kept his own house, he has been here ever since. We're very comfortable with each other. I talk about my husband, he talks about Ida, and it just works. We both know we've had the loves of our lives. We accept that. But we love each other in our own way.'

So how aware was Rene on getting together with Eric of his stellar career as a footballer?

'I wasn't really, to be honest. I knew he had been Brighton's goalkeeper. Other than that, nothing. It was only later when we were at his house and I saw all the memorabilia around the place, which he's kept, that it began to sink in. When we meet people, even after all these years, it's still a topic of conversation. I had to go to hospital three or four years ago to have an examination, and while speaking to one of the nurses she happened to say, "Oh, I know Brighton, and I know Eric Gill." I'm not sure how old she was but she'd heard of him. Wherever we go, there's no avoiding it. But I think that's nice. After all, who doesn't want to be remembered?'

'Old age is an excellent time for outrage.' So said the late American novelist and literary critic Louis Kronenberger. One morning Dave awoke (always a bonus, when you're in your senior years) and decided he and Jackie were going to do something tantamount to outrageous given they (a) lived in safe, suburban Surrey, and (b) were now in their mid-to-late seventies. They were going to up sticks and move house.

'Things were getting so congested in Guildford,' Dave recollects. 'We'd lived in busy areas before – take

Newcastle, for example – but this felt different. We were right in between the university, the hospital and a school, and all of them felt like they were generating more and more traffic. It was bedlam. So one morning I turned to Jackie and said, "Okay, come on, we're moving." And we did – back to Sussex! Back to beside the sea, back to where Jackie was originally from, back to where I'd started my professional career as a goalkeeper. And the difference was instantaneous. All that sea air just does something to you. I'm asthmatic. Not a severe asthmatic, but I am asthmatic. Since I've been back in Sussex, I haven't touched my nebuliser at all. We're in a cul-de-sac in a place called Ovingdean, just along the coast from Brighton, with the sea at the end of the road … and it's marvellous.'

Just five miles separate Ovingdean from Peacehaven, where Eric and Rene live, along the cliff face rollercoaster of a road that is the A259. After all this time, Eric and Dave are very nearly neighbours again. What's more, getting on for 60 years after he'd last played in goal for Brighton & Hove Albion, Dave was amazed to discover that people actually knew his name.

'The spectators were always amazing at Brighton,' he says. 'The club had been through a hell of a lot in the years since we'd left the area. They'd reached the top division, the Premier League as it's now called, and an FA Cup Final, only to fall away and nearly go out of business altogether. At one point they didn't even have a ground. Despite everything, the supporters had always stuck with them. By the time we moved back they had a brand-new ground and were in the Premier League. Things were on the up. People were wearing replica Brighton shirts around town with pride – and they wanted to stop and talk to you! One day I went to exchange my car, which I'd had for around 15 years, at a local garage. I'm not sure if my wife let the cat out of the bag but the reaction was unbelievable. You had all these people coming out of the offices and the mechanics coming out of the repair shop, and they all knew I'd played for the Albion 50 or 60 years ago. That's the quality of the spectators. At Newcastle, the fans are unbelievable but they've always had a fair amount of success. I know some of them might disagree with me about that but compared to Brighton, who didn't have a ground to call home, they have. At Brighton, the fans have not only been remarkably loyal, they've been remarkably loyal in their thousands.'

On returning to the Brighton area, Dave and Jackie took a leaf out of Eric and Rene's book and became fully paid-up members of the indoor bowls club on Denton Island, situated in the very lower reaches of the River Ouse within sight of the English Channel. It was here, on the morning of Wednesday, 12 February 2020, that Dave met up with Eric and Rene to play in an inter-club match.

Only one person was allowed to touch the jack. Only one person was allowed to touch the mat. All the chairs were arranged six feet apart. Everyone, bar Dave, what with his asthma, wore face masks. Best be on the safe side, especially given the average age of the club's members, what with this strange disease, bug, virus, infection, call it what you will, making its way from Asia into mainland Europe. Match completed and, after a round of tea, Eric and Dave went their separate ways until the next time.

Within a matter of days, Dave and Jackie were relaxing 800-odd miles away on the banks of Lake Como. The holiday had long since been booked and at no time did anyone suggest northern Italy was off-limits to tourists. It seemed safe. At least it did to begin with.

'When we went down in the mornings for breakfast, or for meals in the evenings, there were these great long tables in the dining room for everyone to sit at,' recalls Dave. 'One morning we went for breakfast and one of these tables was completely empty. I said to the waiter, "What's going on with that table?" and he replied, "They're all ill." At that very moment I thought, *Uh-oh, something really serious is going on here.* Then, on the way home to England, Jackie became ill. She had all the symptoms of the virus – not that we realised it at the time, of course, because we didn't really know what Covid was at that stage. She didn't have a test, as tests weren't available then. Over time she steadily improved and did eventually have a test, which was negative. But, even now, she still has a cough and some of the symptoms of what they're calling long Covid. With hindsight, I'm convinced that she had it.'

Back in Ovingdean, mindful of Jackie's condition and remembering his brother John's brush with death on returning from China in 2017, Dave drank in the increasingly disturbing news reports as February turned to March, all the while growing more and more alarmed at the apparent lack of urgency shown by those supposedly in power. Day by day, so the number of confirmed Covid-19 cases in the UK rose, followed, as of 5 March, by the first death. Bit by bit, Britain began closing down of its own accord rather than wait for any edict from on high. During the Second World War, Dave couldn't help but remember, Britain had benefited from strong leadership and, thus, defeated the baddies who'd trained their machine guns on him that afternoon in the back garden in Guildford. Where was that kind of leadership now?

Finally, on 23 March – with the death toll already into the hundreds – came the Prime Minister's message from 10 Downing Street: 'From this evening, I must give the British people a very simple instruction – you must stay at home.'

'I think the expression "asleep at the wheel" comes to mind,' declares Dave. 'I mean, why wait until people are going down like ninepins before stepping in? We're into a different era now in terms of world politics and the leaders we have, and it's not a particularly good one. That's my take on it. We'd stayed at home pretty much from the moment we got back from Lake Como. Then again, we're retired – we don't have the pressure of having to go out to work or deciding whether we can work from home. We live in a relaxed cul-de-sac a couple of minutes from the sea. Imagine having to go through the pandemic in a high-rise flat in the middle of a city. In that respect we were very, very fortunate. On a personal note, it was John, my brother, who I was most worried about. When he came back from Beijing his main organs shut down due to whatever it was that he'd picked up out there. If it wasn't for the fact that he lives so close to the Chelsea and Westminster Hospital in London, and the excellent doctors who work there, then he wouldn't have made it through. His immune system and his heart has struggled ever since.'

Blackouts. Air raid sirens. Air raid shelters. Gas masks. Evacuations. Growing up in Britain during the Second World War, there were tangible steps you could take to protect yourself from the Nazi threat. This time it was different. This time the enemy was invisible, not flying in the skies above you or poised on the opposite side of the English Channel ready to invade. This time, other than stocking up with cartloads of toilet rolls, there really was very little you could do except avoid all non-essential contact with other people, largely by staying at home. Nevertheless, it was here that Dave's grounding in sport, more so than his experiences of the Second World War, came to the fore.

'Athletes always tend to think like athletes,' says Dave. 'There's a discipline, a mindset, which sticks with you long after you've finished playing football, rugby, netball or whatever. I was an athlete. Jackie was an athlete, having been involved in sport all her life. For us, when Covid arrived, it was simply a case of thinking like an athlete. For instance, don't go into areas where you could be vulnerable. Do what exercise you can. When you do go shopping, take the sanitiser to wash your hands and a spray to use on the trolleys. Being asthmatic, I couldn't wear a mask, so I had one of those little cards to put round my neck, telling people that I was exempt. Of course you're worried, of course you're concerned, of course you're thinking, *I hope someone hurries up and invents a cure*, but in the meantime you do what you have to do to get through. That's the discipline. Common sense prevails. It has to, or you're in trouble.'

The 'discipline' also meant going without seeing friends, including Eric and Rene. Everyone was at risk from Covid-19, yet some were patently more at risk than others. Eric and Dave might think like two men considerably younger than they are, but there's no escaping the dates on their birth certificates. 'It's just not worth the risk,' is how Eric put it at one stage during the pandemic. At least they had telephones to keep in touch, which they did regularly, their conversations fuelled by the somewhat surreal prospect of a book being written about their lives and enduring friendship. ('Do you think anyone would really want to read about us?' Eric had asked, somewhat sceptically. 'You know what? I think they just might,' went Dave's reply.)

Other than that, the closest Eric and Dave came to being in the same room at the same time for almost two years was while receiving their Covid vaccines and booster jabs at the Brighton Centre, better known as a live music venue. Where once The Jam played their very last gig as a band in December of 1982, so local people queued in their thousands each day for salvation rather than entertainment. Born as they were in 1930 and 1938, respectively, Eric and Dave were among the first to roll up their sleeves after it opened as a vaccination centre in January 2021.

'Walk straight in, follow all the painted lines telling you where to go, into your arm with the needle, and walk straight out again,' says Eric. 'It was marvellous. I don't like what we've been through but, again, as with so many things in my life, I count myself lucky. I've got Rene and she's made sure I do all the things I'm supposed to do. She's been like a double insurance for me. As long as we stick to the rules, we should be okay – that's the way we looked at it and, touch wood, we have been. We kept our distance, kept our masks on and stayed away from crowds. I also count my blessings that we live where we live. The thought of going through all this where I grew up in London ... God almighty! The best thing I ever did was to come down to this part of the world. We've only got to step outside our front door and we're on the seafront, so we've been able to do our walks. And we like our walks, me and Rene. And we walk. We don't stroll. We get a move on. It does us good. I know I don't have a good word to say about Billy Lane these days – the man has no father as far as I'm concerned – but signing for Brighton really did change my entire life. In that respect, I suppose I do have him to thank. He was the one who brought me here, so it all worked out for the best in the end.'

There's a pause. Whatever comes next, you can't help but sense, is either going to be deep, or significant, or both.

'Honestly, I look at my life sometimes and can't help but think I've had more luck than I should have. It's almost as if I've had my luck along with somebody else's as well. I've been at the right place at the right time my entire life, and I swear it hasn't always been down to me. I've just been lucky.'

Compared to Dave, Eric's faith in our political masters and systems of government evaporated long before parts of the world began experimenting with 21st-century populist leaders. Born during Stanley's Baldwin's third term in office, Eric watched as Neville Chamberlain, Winston Churchill, Clement Attlee, Anthony Eden, Harold Macmillan, Alec Douglas-Home and umpteen other Prime Ministers of the UK passed through Downing

Street. Some of its more recent incumbents weren't even born when he was keeping goal for Brighton & Hove Albion. Left, right or centre, experience has told him they all flatter to deceive.

Nope, from where Eric stands, it's people who have the power ... if only they knew it.

'Politicians, they're a different breed altogether,' he asserts. 'You can't ever get to the bottom of them. I've no doubt some good people go into politics but it always ends up the same – the party comes first. They make sure everyone toes the line and says the right party things. Because of that, I'm really not very interested in politics. Looking after myself and my family, that's my priority. I think if everybody did that, then we'd all be better off, not just individually, but collectively. Focus on your family, your loved ones and those closest to you, and it spreads out from there. The more people realise that, the better. That's the way I look at it.'

You grow up living through a war that costs millions of lives worldwide and displaces millions more. You spend what's likely to be a fair chunk of your final years living through a pandemic that costs millions of lives worldwide and leaves millions more dealing with its long-term effects. Two extremely well-lived, eventful lives bookended by two unimaginable horrors.

Still, what doesn't beat you only makes you stronger, as they say. Except that second, more recent bookend could yet prove to be more ruinous than the first.

'At least the war stopped,' says Dave. 'There was a lot of clearing up to do afterwards, but it did stop. This ... this probably won't end because of all the different

Covid variants. It will keep on reoccurring. It will keep on coming back. That's the challenge we are all going to have to learn to live with.'

14

'WE WUNT BE DRUV'

*'Old age isn't so bad when you consider the
alternative.'* – Maurice Chevalier

WE'RE BACK at the indoor bowls club on Denton
Island in Sussex, a world within a world within a world.
It's Thursday, 3 February 2022, nine days short of two
years since Eric and Dave last met face to face. This time
the chairs aren't arranged six feet apart. People are shaking
hands. Some, but not all, are wearing face masks. Jovial
yet far from cavalier – that's the overriding mood as club
members and their guests, for the time being at least, take
advantage of their new-found relative freedom.

Today, Eric and Dave have been joined by Rene and
Jackie, along with Steve Gill and Debby, Steve's wife. Also
present is Brian Powney, Eric and Dave's Brighton & Hove
Albion goalkeeping successor, a resident of the nearby
town of Seaford. The post-match mugs of tea are flowing,
as indeed are the stories. Brian's career as a professional
goalkeeper was curtailed in ruthless style by Brian Clough
during the latter's spell as Brighton manager between

November 1973 and July 1974. As such, he's no fan of Old Big 'Ead, as Clough was sometimes known, and says as much, which in turn gets Eric and Dave going about their own turbulent encounters with Clough the player.

Gradually, the club empties until there's no one left but them and Tina, the keyholder. Still the stories keep coming.

Steve recalls when Dave and Jackie used to babysit him and his brother Malcolm, allowing Eric and Ida time out together. 'The thing I remember about Dave is he would always have a comb in his pocket,' says Steve. 'He'd be combing his hair and looking in the mirror, because he was a good-looking lad, was Dave, quite keen about his appearance. We'd have a laugh and a joke about that, in a nice way.' Everyone smiles as Dave, still sporting a good head of hair, graciously takes another comb-related ribbing.

They talk about the players they once knew, opponents as well as team-mates. They talk about the players no longer with us and the vicious toll of dementia. Dave tells a hilarious tale about the time Brighton faced Preston North End in the FA Cup and were taken apart by Tom Finney, one of the most talented English wingers ever to play the game. 'He could dribble with both feet, which kind of made him twice the player,' Dave recollects. 'Our centre-half, Roy Jennings, came in at half-time and said to Billy Lane, "I'm sorry boss, but I just don't know where he's going!"'

They talk about their favourite football grounds, some long since consigned to the history books. 'I always quite liked the ones where the goals were close to the crowd, like The Dell down at Southampton,' says Eric. 'I remember playing there once and Frankie Howard, our left-winger, who wasn't a very big fellow, stepped back to take a corner ... and somebody leaned over the rail, grabbed him and lifted him up! That still makes me laugh. Just wonderful.'

They talk about the perils of being a goalkeeper. Dave recounts an eye-watering incident when Andy Lochhead, the bulwark-like Scottish centre-forward, smashed a volley straight into his nether regions during a Burnley versus Newcastle encounter. Everyone winces except Jackie, who has a story to match. 'I was watching from the stands one time at Brighton when an opponent shoved Dave as he went up for the ball, crushing him into the goalpost between his legs,' she recalls. 'This little chap ran on with a bucket and cold sponge. Out came the shorts and down went the sponge. Someone sat nearby said, "What's he doing there then?" And this wag went, "They're counting them to make sure they are all there!" Everyone around us just roared with laughter. I tell you what though – it's just as well they were, otherwise neither of our daughters would have been born!'

The following day, Dave turned 84 years old. He's not exactly sure how this has happened (wasn't it 1960 only a few months ago?) but he's glad it has. 'Every now and then, maybe when I stand up or go to walk somewhere, I might take a little stumble or just catch my foot on something,' he says. 'I suppose that's nature's way of reminding me that I'm not 21 anymore and to watch what I'm doing. I am at the stage in life now when I wake up in the morning and think to myself, *Bloody hell, I'm still here!* Honestly, I do that, because so many of them aren't here anymore. But I'll tell you what, I'm nothing on Eric.'

In what way?

'Well, the man is amazing. I'll give you an example. Not long after we moved back to Sussex from Guildford, we came out of the bowls club one day and I happened to mention that I didn't have a map of Brighton. I said to Eric, "I'm going to have to get one because I've forgotten all the streets." He goes, "Hold on a minute," sprints across the car park, finds a spare map in his car and sprints back again. "Here's one," he says. And I'm standing there, open-mouthed … because he's just SPRINTED! In what must have been his 90th year! I couldn't believe it.'

In Eric and Dave's adopted county of Sussex, there's a saying: 'We wunt be druv'. It dates back to the 19th century and, having seemingly gone into hibernation throughout much of the 20th century, has returned with a vengeance in more recent times. Roughly translated, it's Sussex dialect for 'we will not be driven'. Other, looser, more modern interpretations have been known to include 'don't mess with me/us', 'back off', 'up yours' and 'f*** off' but essentially the underlying vibe is that Sussex folk are independent of mind and won't take kindly to being pushed around.

As affable, entertaining and well-mannered as Eric Gill and Dave Hollins are, 'we wunt be druv' encapsulates both men perfectly in terms of their zest and approach to life. They will talk until the cows come home around all manner of subjects but, if they don't agree with you, then they'll say so – politely, yet firmly. Likewise, don't expect them to do anything they don't particularly want to do.

There's also something of a 'Mod' mentality about Eric and Dave. Besides adopting Brighton as a spiritual home over the years, 'Mods' were renowned for revering the music and fashion of the past while living in the present. As much as the past constitutes so much of their lives, Eric and Dave live in the here and now. They remember the Second World War. They remember rationing. Eric, for one, remembers slum housing. By no stretch of the imagination was the past a better place, as one particularly disturbing incident from Dave's childhood amply demonstrates.

'Kids in our day had an immense amount of freedom compared to the kids of today,' says Dave. 'When I was young, we'd go out bird-watching or whatever. Your mum would make you sandwiches and off you'd go under your own steam from sunrise to sunset. Today, kids aren't even allowed to walk to school on their own. As a society, we've become so paranoid. On the other hand, we do talk more openly now. We're willing to discuss things that perhaps we weren't back then, which I think is a huge positive. Once, when I was at school, our history teacher told me to put the books away in the cupboard and, while I was doing it, he touched my backside. At the time, I thought nothing of it … but I still remember it all these years later. It stayed with me. If that happened now, I'd like to think it would get reported and the perpetrator would be dealt with.'

On a more light-hearted note both Eric and Dave continue to be amazed, not to mention flattered, by the attention they receive from football followers, especially considering how long it's been since they stopped playing. Just before the start of the 2021/22 season, Eric was voted

Guildford City's best-ever goalkeeper in a poll of the club's supporters. A few months prior to the Covid-19 outbreak, one of Surrey's more esteemed auction houses also reported brisk business when Dave's collection of international goalkeeping jerseys went under the hammer.

'Money is the governing body of life itself,' confides Dave as to why he decided to part with them. 'One day I turned the television on and heard that poor Gordon Banks had died. I thought, *Well, this jumper that I've got under glass, complete with the programme from the Wales versus England game of 1963, could well be worth a lot of money.* I had four of them to sell – Gordon's, one of my own Welsh ones, Gilmar's from my first trip to South America and an Irish jumper, which I'd swapped after a game with Bobby Irvine, their goalkeeper. I thought, *I've got two daughters – they won't really want them.* They were pretty big, these framed shirts, and took up a fair bit of room. So I decided to get rid of them. The Gordon Banks one in particular went for quite a lot of money. I'm almost certain it ended up in the Stoke City museum, which I think is brilliant. That's the right place for it.'

As for Dave's collection of international caps? They, he maintains, are going nowhere.

'Those are the most valuable material things that I own. I shall treasure them forever. They are special because every single one of them is a memory. Every country I played against is itemised on the actual caps themselves. I look at the Brazil one from the South American tour of 1962 and it's a memory. I look at the England one of 1963 and it's a memory. I look at the Italy one and I'm in Tuscany getting ready to face them in Florence. I look at them all and I remember the places we went to and the people I played alongside and indeed against. Men like John Charles. To think that I got to share a room with one of the greatest players of all time – and he was such a nice bloke as well, was John. I could never part with those caps because it would be like being parted from those memories.'

Individually, Eric and Dave enjoyed distinguished careers as goalkeepers that, in their old age, they look back on with immense pride. Chances are they would have enjoyed those distinguished careers had they never met. Eric was, after all, a local hero at Brighton & Hove Albion prior to Dave making his professional debut. Both men, however, certainly raised their games as a result of being around one another. Dave, with his fresh-faced enthusiasm, not to mention outstanding ability, kept Eric on his toes for years. No chance of any complacency setting in with a reserve goalkeeper like that around the place. In turn, Dave benefited from studying Eric close up, learning first-hand from one of Britain's leading goalkeeping exponents of the 1950s.

Football aside, Eric and Dave also believe they became better men as a consequence of meeting and becoming friends.

'Eric showed me the way, not just as a goalkeeper but as a person,' declares Dave. 'I wanted to be like him. He was a lovely man. He still is a lovely man. And Ida was a lovely woman, too. I used to think to myself, *If I ever meet someone, I'd like it to be just like it is with Eric and Ida*. And when I met Jackie, it was. What's more, Jackie and Ida hit it off from the start as well, which only made things easier. Our friendship has been like a marriage really. Although we didn't speak for some time while I was at Newcastle, he's always been there for me, just as I hope I've always been there for him. As soon as we moved back to Brighton, the first person to ring was Eric. That's true friendship.'

'Well that's very nice of him to say,' replies Eric with a smile. 'I think we were cut from the same cloth, Dave and me, and I don't just mean in terms of being goalkeepers. He's a lovely guy and Jackie has always been a lovely wife. He also cares about people. The one thing I really don't like to see in this world is injustice, and I think Dave feels very much the same way. I don't like it when people are browbeaten or lose out through no fault of their own. You almost want someone to come along and say, "No, that's unfair, that's not going to happen," but of course life doesn't work like that. I've been lucky but a lot of people suffer from awful bad luck. You get some where nothing ever seems to go right for them. That, for me, is a tragedy. I do care, yes, and Dave does too. It's in his nature. The more people who cared, the better off we'd all be.'

The years roll by. Association football as a form of entertainment continues to consist of 22 people at any given time attempting to put a ball into one of two goals situated at either end of a pitch. That bit hasn't changed since Eric made his professional debut in goal for Charlton Athletic away to Manchester United in September 1951.

It's what happens off the field that bears little if any resemblance to the post-war game Eric and Dave initially fell in love with.

In October 2021, in a deal reputed to be worth £305m, ownership of Newcastle United passed into the hands of a Saudi Arabia-led consortium. On paper, the Magpies had become the richest club in the world. And to think the £11,000 they once splashed out to bring Dave from Brighton to Tyneside was considered a lot of money.

Just short of a month after the deal was completed, Newcastle made the long trip south to take on Brighton in a Premier League fixture. Dave, having had a foot in both camps, was invited along as Albion's special guest. On the one hand, he was fully jabbed. On the other, with large numbers of people returning to football matches in England after the Covid-enforced absence, approximately 30,000 other souls would in all likelihood be there with him. Risky, you could say.

Then again, in your eighties, time is short. No point staying close to home forever. Anyway, despite being on a Saturday, it was a night match. And, as anyone who's ever attended a night match will tell you, they're special. The pitch always seems so much greener. The sound always seems so much sharper. To paraphrase Frankie Valli and his Four Seasons, the night turns your head around. Whether you're 8 or 88, that never changes. Dave decided he would go.

Saturday, 6 November came. Night fell. The car parks around the Amex Stadium began to fill. The stands began to fill. The hospitality areas began to fill, including the one where Dave entertained supporters young enough to be his grandchildren, maybe even his great-grandchildren, with stories throughout the evening. At some point he was introduced to Gordon Smith, another former Brighton player. To Gordon's chagrin, all many people want to talk to him about is his infamous miss against Manchester United in the 1983 FA Cup Final (which, to add insult to injury, would almost certainly have won Brighton the cup, coming as it did in the last minute of extra time with the score at 2-2). Not Dave, bowled over instead by Gordon's ability to speak German fluently. 'Such an eloquent lad,' he later enthuses.

At some point close to kick-off time both Dave and Gordon swapped the hospitality lounges for the pitch itself to be interviewed live in front of the gathering masses. Gordon spoke about the marked differences between the all-singing, all-dancing Amex Stadium and the basic yet charismatic Goldstone Ground, bulldozed in 1997 and now the site of a retail park. Dave recalled his playing days at both Brighton and Newcastle, hitting the right notes with all four sides of the ground, including the packed away end.

Then came the tangent in the proceedings.

'I was wondering if I could just say a few words about Eric Gill?' Dave suddenly asked his interviewer, pushing on without so much as waiting for a reply. 'Eric Gill played 247 consecutive games for the Albion back in the 1950s when I was his understudy. He's a lovely guy and, even better, he turned 91 last Wednesday. I think that deserves a cheer.'

At which point the third-biggest cheer of the evening sounded around the Amex Stadium prior to Brighton and Newcastle playing out a 1-1 draw, a fitting result perhaps, given Dave's allegiances.

The following day, Dave telephoned his old friend and told him what he'd done.

'That's brilliant!' said Eric. 'But I tell you what – you're going to have to do it again when I get to 100.'

ERIC'S PEARLS OF WISDOM

Advice to young goalkeepers

When I was young, I used to go and watch goalkeepers play, just to see what they did. Then I tried to copy all the good ones. That would be my advice. And if you can't go, maybe because it's a bit pricey, then watch them on television. I used to go to Chelsea whenever I could to watch Vic Woodley play. He was my big hero. He always seemed to do everything right. It looked like it came naturally to him, although he probably worked hard at it. He just had this knack of knowing where the ball was going to go and getting his body behind it. Find your very own Vic Woodley, watch them, and learn from them.

The secret to living a long, largely happy life

Luck undoubtedly plays its part, as I've said many times. I was born lucky, I'll tell you that – everything in my life I've had through luck. But, in general, I think so much depends on the people who are close to you. By that, I mean your wife or your partner. If that's good, if that's solid, then you can face anything. I've been lucky. In my time, I've had both – a wife and a partner – and they've been wonderful. It just takes all the worry away. Find a good one, in other words.

DAVE'S PEARLS OF WISDOM

Advice to young goalkeepers

I'm not entirely sure that I'm qualified to offer advice to young goalkeepers these days. The position has changed so much. As I've said, they are more like sweepers or ice hockey goaltenders than the goalkeepers of my day. They play with their feet as much as their hands. That's the way coaching has gone. Then there's the way the ball moves – it swerves, rather than comes at you directly. However, some things, in my opinion, don't change. First, there's the importance of knowing where you are in your goal. What markers do you have that help you to do your job and get your positioning right? For me, it was always the penalty spot, the near post and the far post. Always have those markers in mind. Never lose your bearings. Second, never lose focus. You've got to be concentrating all the time. Third, and this is linked in many ways to my second point, always keep your eye on the ball. The ball can make a fool of you if you don't know where it is, so watch it all the time, even when it goes out of play. It's all about the ball.

The secret to living a long, largely happy life

I'm probably half a stone overweight, compared to when I was playing. What I'm saying, in a roundabout way, is it's

278

all down to who you marry or settle down with. Choose carefully and hope they choose you back! My wife has a great sense of humour – she needs one to live with me – and she's very smart. But, yes, eating well also helps. Her food is incredible. Look after yourself and watch what you put inside you. I also benefited from good advice as a kid. For that, I have my parents, in particular my father, to thank. Don't be afraid to listen and take that advice as and when it comes. And exercise. I don't go over the top, especially not at my age, but I don't sit down all day either. A little bit of exercise, even if it's only walking, does you good.

ACKNOWLEDGEMENTS

WRITING A book, if you excuse the sporting analogy, is very much a team effort. You need good people around you to provide help, advice, quotes, statistics, background information, specialist knowledge, local knowledge, constructive criticism, pictures, designs, cups of tea and the occasional ale when the sun goes down and the creative juices cease to flow. If you haven't got a team, there's no book. It's as simple as that.

Writing this particular book, as delightful as Eric Gill and Dave Hollins are, hasn't always been easy. Traditional sources of information, for instance public libraries, were often closed due to the Covid-19 pandemic. Face-to-face interviews, at least initially, were out of the question, again due to the pandemic. To use that old NASA adage from the days when men went to the Moon, I, we, worked the problem. And we got there. And it's been fun getting there.

First and foremost, thank you to Eric and Dave for telling their stories, individual and shared. It's been a privilege, gentlemen, and I only hope I've done you justice. Thanks also to Irene Taylor, Eric's partner, and Jackie Hollins, Dave's wife, for their support (and regular prodding!) throughout both the writing and research process.

At the southern end of England a big tip of the hat goes to Tim Carder, Ian Hine, Luke Nicoli and Paul Hazlewood for their help on the Brighton & Hove Albion front. At the northern end of England further tips of that very same hat are due to Nick Barnes, Chris Emmerson, Jon Harle and Paul Joannou for their invaluable help when it came to Newcastle United and the city of Newcastle in general. Across the space, and football clubs, in between I'm heavily indebted to Paul Taylor at Mansfield Town, Pete Stanford at Aldershot Town, Ben Hayes and Paul Baker at Charlton Athletic and Stuart Phillips and Barry Underwood at Guildford City, who all set aside time to answer my various questions and provide additional material. In Wales, Ceri Stennett, Geraint Jenkins and Ian Garland were also a big help when it came to filling in the gaps surrounding Dave's international career.

On the playing front, or rather ex-playing front, I'd like to give a big hand to Charlie Baker, Frank Clark, the late Denis Foreman, Steve Gill, Cliff Jones, the late Nobby Lawton, Trevor Porter, Brian Powney, the late Dave Sexton, the late John Shepherd, Adrian Thorne and Andrew Wycichowski for sharing their memories while writing this book and, on occasion, in previous interviews I'd conducted that produced relevant source material.

Thank you to the journalists who went before me in terms of producing match reports and features, which proved extremely useful in helping to tell Eric and Dave's stories, especially those tied to the *Daily Telegraph*, the *Evening Argus*, the *Nottingham Evening Post*, the *Northern*

Echo, *The Times*, the *Western Mail* and the wonderfully named *Mansfield Chad*. To access some of those, time was spent at the mines of information that are Cathays Library in Cardiff and The Keep in Brighton. Tony Brown, guardian of the (English) National Football Archive, was also a big help when it came to clarifying match appearances and statistics.

Closer to home, my partner Jane and children Rhiannon and Luca deserve long-service medals for sharing their lives with a freelance writer and all that entails. Thanks also to Paul Hayward, Dave Purcel and Denton Island Bowls Club for adding bells and whistles to the finished article.

Finally, Pitch, as in the publishers, in particular Jane Camillin, Duncan Olner, Ivan Butler, Dean Rockett and Graham Hales. The last, and probably the best, of the independents, certainly when it comes to sport.

BIBLIOGRAPHY

Brown, Craig. *One, Two, Three, Four: The Beatles in Time* (4th Estate, 2020).
Carder, Tim & Harris, Roger. *Albion A–Z: A Who's Who of Brighton & Hove Albion* (Goldstone Books, 1997).
Chrisp, Peter. *Britain Since 1930* (BBC Fact Finders, 1994).
Greaves, Jimmy. *The Heart of the Game* (Time Warner Books, 2005).
Greaves, Jimmy & Giller, Norman. *Don't Shoot the Manager* (Boxtree, 1993).
Hazlewood, Nick. *In the Way! Goalkeepers: A Breed Apart* (Mainstream Publishing, 1996).
Hutchings, Steve & Nawrat, Chris. *The Sunday Times Illustrated History of Football* (Ted Smart, 1994).
Joannou, Paul. *United: The First 100 Years* (ACL & Polar Publishing, 1991).
McKinstry, Leo. *Jack & Bobby* (HarperCollins, 2003).
Rollins, Jack. *History of Aldershot Football Club* (published by the author, 1975).
Soar, Phil. *The Illustrated Encyclopaedia of British Football* (WHSmith, 1989).
Williams, Michael. *Steaming to Victory: How Britain's Railways Won the War* (Arrow Books, 2014).

Films/Documentaries
Blackball (Midfield Films, 2003).
Brighton Rock (Charter Film Productions, 1947).
Ripping Yarns: Golden Gordon (BBC, 1979).

Online Resources
www.bbc.co.uk
www.hmsdunedin.co.uk
www.thecityground.com
www.seagullsprogrammes.co.uk
www.sportspsychologist.com
www.youtube.com

INDEX

INDEX

INDEX

Also available at all good book stores

9781801501255

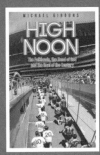
9781785317828

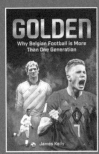
9781801501057

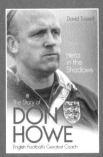
9781801500876

9781801500906

9781801501101

9781801500968

9781801500937

9781801500975